Once Upon A Time:

Elvis and Anita

(Courtesy of Memphis Press-Scimitar)

Once Upon A Time:

Elvis and Anita

Memories of My Mother

By Jonnita Brewer Barrett

BrewBar Publishing
1485 Livingston Ln
Jackson, MS 39213

www.elvisandanita.com

Front cover from Commercial Appeal/Landov

Back cover from the collection of Anita Wood

Library of Congress Control Number : 2012912365

ISBN:978-0-9858056-0-9

Dedication

To my dear mother and late father,

for encouraging me to write this story,

as well as everything else I've ever set out to accomplish.

To my husband for being my support in life,

and for making it happen.

.

ANITA WOOD

WILLIAM MORRIS AGENCY

(Courtesy of Dr. John Carpenter)

Contents

Acknowledgments

This book would not be possible without the help of a lot of people. I hope I have not overlooked anyone.

First and foremost I want to thank Jesus Christ for saving my soul and giving me abundant life. Without Him, I could do nothing.

Nor could I have done this without my mother, Anita Wood. Thank you for sharing your life with me, even when I was driving you insane with questions!

I would be remiss not to thank my husband and family for putting up with me while I was zoned into writing and not at their beck and call.

Of course, my editor, Ed Robertson, was wonderful. He took my sometimes rambling thoughts, organized them and smoothed them over to end up with a flowing, understandable, incredible book. He was also always there for me whenever I asked the question, "What do I do now?" Thank you, Ed, I couldn't have done it without you. (And special thanks to Winifred Golden, for introducing me to you.)

Thank you also to Elvis Presley Enterprises for their cooperation; to Nicole LaBombard, for your helpful suggestions; and to the University of Memphis Library/Special Collections.

A Special Message from Anita Wood Brewer

This book was written from my precious memories through my only daughter, Jonnita Barrett. Her words made me relive some of the most wonderful, and some of the most trying, times I have ever experienced. I was with Elvis when everything seemed new, and life was full to him and everyone in his presence. Elvis and I were home to each other during his rise to superstardom. He was my first love, and I have felt an almost painful connection and overwhelming sense of loyalty to him ever since he came to my door for the very first time. It has not always been logical, but that is the way I feel.

I have shared my memories with my daughter all of her life, but over the last several years we have spent many long hours together discussing my feelings and thoughts about my time with Elvis. Jonnita has pushed me to remember, so that we could all share the wonderful, as well as not so wonderful, moments that he and I shared during our five years together.

I haven't talked about Elvis to the media much over the years. He never wanted me to when we were together (and I have honored his wishes most all my life), nor have I ever wanted to diminish my memories of Elvis in any way. And yet for years, so many people have tried to convince me that I should write a book about our life together, and until now I have always resisted. But with the encouragement of my family, and the persistence of my daughter, I finally decided the time was right to share my memories with you.

It never ceases to amaze me that anyone would still be interested in my experiences with my first love, Elvis Presley. I hope you enjoy reading about us.

Love to her and all my family,

Anita Wood Brewer

ONCE UPON A TIME: ELVIS AND ANITA

Prologue

Christmas 1977

It was bitter cold outside that day, as you might expect for Memphis in the last week of December. The heater in the car was broken, so we bundled ourselves with blankets and huddled as close as we could next to each other throughout the long, two-hour drive. My Aunt Karen was driving. My mother sat beside her up front, while I was in the back with Mamaw [my grandmother]. I was eleven years old at the time. It was a few days after Christmas, and about four months after that sad day in August when we heard the news that Elvis Presley had died. His death had shocked the world, of course — he was so young, he had so much more yet to offer, and it was hard to imagine a world without him in it. Especially for the people who knew him well, like Momma.

My mother, Anita Wood, was Elvis' steady girlfriend from 1957 to 1962, before and after he met Priscilla — and though his handlers (Colonel Parker, especially) went to great pains to downplay their relationship, it's no secret that Elvis loved her, so much so that he invited her to live with him and his family at Graceland, not long after he and Momma met. As much as she wanted to attend the funeral, she couldn't bring herself to go. She knew what a spectacle the press would make of her being there, and she did not want to take any attention away from Elvis. But her heart was with his family that day, and in the weeks and months since. Today was her first opportunity to pay her respects.

As we approached the massive iron gates of Graceland, my grandmother apologized for not taking me there sooner so that I could have met Elvis. I told her it was okay. Besides, I knew that Momma didn't want to hear that conversation right then because her mind was elsewhere.

The man in the gate house approached our car. Momma's face lit up, like he was an old friend. I soon found out he was Uncle Vester, the brother of Elvis' father, Vernon.

"Hey, Anita," said Vester. "It's so good to see you! How are you doing?"

"I'm fine, Vester, thank you," Momma replied. "This is my momma, my daughter, Jonnita, and my sister-in-law, Karen. I came by to see Grandma and Mr. Presley. Are they up there?"

"Yeah, they are," said Vester. "But Priscilla is in town, so I better call up to the house first and make sure it's okay."

At that moment a sense of dread came over Momma, though she managed not to show it. She and Priscilla knew who each other were, of course, but they'd never actually met — and since Momma hadn't anticipated seeing her, she didn't know what to expect.

1

We waited in the car for about a minute before the big gates opened up. As we made our way up the long driveway, a whole wave of emotions swept over Momma: happiness at the familiar sight, but also a deep sadness. After all, Elvis was the life of that house, and without him it seemed so quiet and still.

Priscilla was awaiting us as we pulled in behind the house. She was dressed in a long-sleeved silk shirt, and as we got out of the car, Aunt Karen noticed that she was not wearing any makeup. Yet she looked absolutely stunning.

She walked up to my mom, held out her hand, and introduced herself. "I'm Priscilla. It's so nice to finally meet you."

"I'm Anita," Momma said as she took her hand. "Nice to meet you, too."

Then Priscilla said something I will never forget: "I have heard so much about you, Anita, I feel like I already know you."

I remember feeling awestruck when I heard her say that. It wasn't until much later that I found out that Priscilla used to read Momma's letters to Elvis, trying to find out what Momma was like and what Elvis liked and didn't like. So I guess you could say that she had studied Momma from afar all those years ago.

I stood there looking up at them as they exchanged pleasantries. "Well, you are just so little," Priscilla said to Momma. "How do you stay so slim? Are you on a special diet?"

"No, not really," Momma smiled. "I guess I'm just very fortunate to be able to eat whatever I want."

"Not me," said Priscilla. "I can't have anything but fruits and vegetables — and not even much of that. If I eat anything I'm not supposed to, I will gain weight."

"I'd like to see Mr. Presley, and also Grandma," said Momma. "Would that be all right?"

"Of course," said Priscilla. She was very gracious. "He's in the office. Why don't you go over and see him there, then I'll wait for you in the house with Grandma."

* * *

We went to the office, a huge room back behind the house, where all the fan mail was located. I had never seen so much mail in my life, before or since. There were just stacks and stacks of it all over the place.

The first person we saw was Patsy, Elvis's double first cousin. Patsy became very close friends with Momma when she lived at Graceland, and often invited Momma to spend the night at her own house when Elvis was away. Patsy was as grounded as could be, and Momma loved her company. They gave each other a big, warm embrace and talked for several minutes before Momma introduced the rest of us.

Vernon must have heard all that commotion, because it wasn't long before he popped out of his office and ambled over to Momma. "Why, Anita, it's good to see you," he said with a hug. "How ya doing? You look so good."

"It's good to see you, too," she said. "I am so sorry about Elvis. We all miss him so much. I didn't come to the funeral because Elvis wasn't there, and I didn't want to fool with all that press. If it had been someone else in the family, I would have come for Elvis. But I did say a prayer for y'all, because I knew how hard it would be for y'all. He was so young and this was so unexpected."

Mr. Presley began to tear up. "I understand, Anita... and yes, it was very hard on everyone. The press was asking everything and the number of people there was crazy."

They continued talking for a while, reliving memories. "Weren't you supposed to come to Germany with us, when Elvis was stationed there?" he said.

"Yes, I was," said Momma, "but Colonel Parker put a stop to that. He thought if I came over there, the press would assume we were married, and that would be bad for Elvis' career. Wasn't that silly?"

"Yeah, I suppose it was," said Mr. Presley. "But Elvis had to do whatever Colonel Parker told him to do for his career back then."

Then he paused a bit and looked at Momma wistfully. "You were always very understanding about things like that, Anita."

That made Momma feel really good, and for a moment she found herself back in time, thinking about the many long conversations she had with him and Gladys, Elvis' mother. Gladys was about the straightest shooter my mother had ever known. Momma used to tell her how inadequate she felt at first about being Elvis' girlfriend, especially with all the photographs she saw in the newspapers of him with other girls. Gladys put her right at ease: "Don't you worry about that, Anita. Elvis has to pretend he likes those other girls because the Colonel wants him to. But you're the one he wants. Don't ever forget it."

Gladys was always very convincing, and my mom believed she meant what she said.

* * *

Momma talked some more with Mr. Presley, and then they said their goodbyes. He gave her another big hug, and we all went back to the house to see Grandma.

When we walked inside, the first thing Momma noticed was a room that had not been there when she lived at Graceland. It was called the Jungle Room, and as you can imagine, it looked like a jungle, with a wild green carpet that ran along the floor and ceiling and even along the walls in the hallway. I had never seen anything remotely like it before, and neither had Momma.

Then we saw Lisa Marie, sitting at the same bar where Momma had seen Elvis sit so many times before. She gave my mom quite a start when she looked up at her.

"You look just like your daddy," Momma said. "You really do! I'm Anita, and I am so sorry about your daddy. But I just want you to know, you look just like him. It's really breathtaking."

Lisa gave her a smile, but didn't say anything. She was nine at the time, two years younger than me. I felt so sorry for her. I couldn't imagine losing my daddy at her age, like she had. I wanted to play with her, but she was extremely shy. She looked at me and gave a little smile, too, then excused herself and left. She really did look like her daddy, only with blonde hair.

We made our way down the hall and found Grandma in Mr. and Mrs. Presley's old bedroom. She was sitting in her rocking chair, dipping snuff and watching television with Priscilla. Momma loved Grandma so much, it brought tears to her eyes just seeing her.

"Oh, Neeter," Grandma said, "it's so good to see you." They gave each other a long hug, then Momma introduced us. Grandma could not believe that I was my momma's daughter. She continued to chat with us for a while before she and Momma got to talking.

My mom can become very animated when she's fully engaged in a conversation — she speaks with her eyes as well as with words, and often uses hand gestures to emphasize her thoughts. Before long, she was sitting at Grandma's feet as they reminisced about the old days, how Momma would sleep with her when Elvis was gone, the time they spent together in Texas, and how she wished Momma had been in Germany with them, "especially because they didn't have any good television on over there."

At that moment, Grandma motioned to Priscilla and asked if she and Momma had met. "Yes, Ma'am," my mom laughed, and then she and Grandma carried on as if they were the only ones in the room. Priscilla kept her eyes on Momma, while we kept our eyes on Priscilla (Aunt Karen still could not believe how naturally beautiful she was).

* * *

At some point Priscilla invited us to tour Graceland while Grandma and Momma talked. We said sure. Aunt Karen and Mamaw were shown the rest of the house, but I was left standing in the hall. The house was enormous to me, with so many ornate decorations. I was afraid to touch anything, so I wandered around aimlessly by myself.

Momma had told me many stories about Graceland, but this was the first time I'd ever seen it. She often described it as a castle straight out of a fairy tale, and I could easily see why: everything was so perfectly in place, it almost seemed

4

like no one had lived there. There was lots of gold, red and white. From the front door the dining room was the first room on the left, with an antique cabinet full of crystal and beautiful china, and a very long formal dining room table. The living room was on the right, and had a beautiful fireplace with mirrors all around it, plus a huge sectional couch, a large coffee table, and many chairs that were gold, floral and red. A back staircase came from upstairs straight to the kitchen. That staircase will become very significant later on in this story.

I looked out the window and saw Lisa Marie riding around on a golf cart, and again wished I could have played with her. I walked over to the dining room table, and saw more toys on top of there than I had ever seen in one place except at a toy store. Since it was Christmastime, they must have been gifts for Lisa Marie.

Across the foyer I saw a room that was red and white, with lots of white pillows, and a baby grand piano. As I stared at it, I kept picturing Momma sitting there with Elvis, singing and playing.

Many times, I've thought back to that day in 1977, and with each passing year, I kept thinking about the years that Momma spent with Elvis — a time when he was young, carefree and well on his way to becoming a superstar. From what I know of about Elvis, I believe that five-year period, 1957 through 1962, were among the best years of his life. His career had just taken off, he had just bought Graceland, and his mother, Gladys, was still with him. It was a magical time, when life seemed unbelievably good.

Elvis was like a prince who had his choice of all the fair maidens in the land, any one of whom wouldn't hesitate to fall at his feet and worship him. And yet he fell in love with a small-town girl, who at first barely noticed him at all: my mother, Anita Wood. Their life together seemed like a fairy tale at times, which I'm told was often the case with Elvis. But unfortunately not all fairy tales end with a happily ever after.

Well, let me qualify that. Had Momma married Elvis, she would not have married my daddy, and I would not be here talking to you.

Momma has told me many stories about her life with Elvis. He was the first love of her life, and she often looks back at those years as a time filled with laughter, fun, happiness, thrills, tenderness and, as one might expect when one's boyfriend is The King of Rock 'n' Roll, a good dose of craziness. But, as you can also imagine, some of those memories are tinged with the sadness of loss and the hurt of betrayal.

What I'm about to share with you is a story worth telling, a wonderful story with all the elements of a fairy tale, a romance, or a tragedy, depending on your point of view. So, as fairy tales go, let's start at the beginning, or "Once upon a time."

Chapter 1

Once Upon a Time

My mother, Anita Marie Wood, was born in Bells, Tennessee on May 27, 1938, to W.A. and Dorothy Wood. Elvis was born in Tupelo, Mississippi on January 8, 1935, to Vernon and Gladys Presley. He was the only surviving child in his family, while Momma is the oldest child, and only girl, of four stair-step children (her younger brothers are named Jerry, Joe, and Andy). My grandmother had all four children within five years — and as those of you who are moms know, having that many little ones is a very daunting task, especially back then. The U.S. was in the middle of the Great Depression, and life was not working out quite the way that Mamaw had envisioned for herself. She had grown up dirt poor with nine brothers and sisters, and what little they had was shared among each other. The one thing my grandmother could call her own was her dreams, and she always dreamed big.

Dorothy loved W.A., but she married him when she was so young, mostly because she desperately wanted to escape her own humble beginnings. He was the younger of two boys, but as his older brother died in childhood, he basically grew up as an only child. Because of the tragedy of his brother's untimely death, my grandfather's parents were very structured and overprotective with him. Consequently, when he married my grandmother, he expected his household to be run in a certain manner, and his children raised in a certain way, because that was what he knew. Which meant that Mamaw went from her childhood home, where she had nothing, to a married home where she had little freedom or control.

Now don't get me wrong: my grandfather loved my grandmother, and she loved him dearly in return. He was her rock, always solid and steady. He worked two jobs, one on the railroad and the other driving a truck for Gulf Transport, and he always gave her whatever she needed to provide for their children. He just expected things done in a certain way (like having dinner waiting on the table when he got home), and he never veered from that.

W.A. had red hair, which I love because my eldest son does, too. I don't know if the old saying about red-headed men being hot-tempered holds true for all redheads, but it did for my grandfather (and for that matter, my son). Fortunately, Dorothy understood that about him, and she worked hard to keep him happy (and his temper in check).

My mother's family was very conservative, hardworking and family-oriented. Here's a little piece of wisdom that Mamaw taught my mother, and which Momma passed on to me: "No matter if you are in your gown all day, before your husband gets home, get dressed, put on makeup and tidy up the house. Don't let him return home to find you looking just the way he left you — give him a reason to look forward to coming home each day."

Of course, times have changed, and a mother's schedule can be a little more hectic than it was in my mother and grandmother's day. They didn't run kids to soccer, football, baseball, basketball, tennis, softball, track, cheerleading, dance, gymnastics, voice, piano, guitar, and school functions like current-day moms do, not to mention those of us with jobs outside of the home! That said, I think it's really good advice — and while I don't always follow it to the letter, I do try to make my house a place that my husband wants to come home to every day, and I always try to at least be presentable. My husband thinks it's good advice, too. We like to think it's played a small part in why our marriage has worked for more than twenty years.

My grandmother was a great cook — not in the "gourmet magazine" sense, but rather the "when you taste it, it's so good you want more" sense. She cooks good ole Southern food — nothing fancy, with the possible exception of her homemade, "grate your own" coconut cake. Plus her homemade ice cream, fried corn and sweet potatoes are to die for.

Sometimes the simplest things in life are best, and one of my grandmother's favorite pastimes is to play games. So, as you can imagine, eating great meals and playing games together were a regular part of my mother's upbringing, which she in turn passed on to me. Some of my fondest childhood memories include learning to play various games along with my parents, aunts, uncles, and grandparents at various family get-togethers. Sometimes, while the adults played, my cousins and I would put together a play or some kind of variety show for their entertainment. I loved doing this, because the adults would always stop what they were doing and give us their full attention. Mamaw always encouraged performing in her family, so I'm sure that led in some way to my mom becoming a performer.

Unfortunately (or maybe fortunately), I did not inherit my mom's incredible singing talent, or I would have probably followed in her footsteps, despite the fact that neither my mom nor my dad ever encouraged their children to go into any field that might bring about fame. Matter of fact, they strongly discouraged it. (While Momma always enjoyed singing and acting, she never did care for the lifestyle of most entertainers, not to mention the anxiety of performing, especially in a competitive setting. But we'll get to all that later.)

These memories of the times spent with my family are among the most treasured in my life. I am told that we spend money on what is truly important to us; for my grandparents, that meant family. Family time was so important to Dorothy and W.A., they only went into debt twice a year: Christmas and summer vacation, the times most associated with family.

Christmastime was always special when Momma was a child. While the presents were not extravagant, it was the family traditions that made the holiday. Every year she and her brothers would go out in the woods and chop down a cedar tree, because that's the kind of tree that my grandmother wanted. My grandfather would also shoot down some mistletoe from the top of the trees with his shotgun. I remember how much fun we had together when I was a child, when Momma introduced this tradition to me. We would all decorate the tree, hang the mistletoe, and eat a fabulous traditional Christmas feast including turkey and dressing, homemade macaroni and cheese, sweet potatoes with marshmallows, black-eyed peas, green beans, fried corn, homemade yeast rolls, chess pie, coconut cake, chocolate cake and pineapple cake. Then we'd all play games, or put on a performance, until it was time for the little ones to go to bed so that Santa Claus could come by and leave toys while the adults played cards until the wee hours of the morning.

Every summer Momma's family took a vacation — my mother, her brothers, her parents, and her father's parents. (How in the world they all fit in one car, I will never know!) W.A. liked to camp in the mountains, while Dorothy liked the beach. (Most summers, they vacationed at Myrtle Beach, South Carolina, so I guess the beach won out more often.) Sometimes, they'd do something totally different, such as drive across the country and stop at various destinations along the way. By the time I was a little girl, my mother's family preferred to spend summer vacation camping in the mountains of Tennessee, with all the grandkids in tow. I remember cooking over a campfire, picking blackberries along the trails and sleeping in a tent with my grandparents. Momma was afraid of bears though, so she'd sleep in the car along with my little brothers. I remember what fun we always had, playing games, eating good food, and laughing a lot. Momma said our family vacations were much the same as when she was young.

When Momma was still a little girl, her family moved to Jackson, Tennessee. That's when her path in life began to change. It was around this same time that Elvis was given his first guitar (which was when *his* path in life began to change). My grandmother wanted her daughter to have everything she never had, so she encouraged (or, you could say, required) her to sing and act. She enrolled my mom in expression classes, which are like acting classes, as well as giving her voice lessons (even though Momma already had a natural singing voice). Mamaw also believed that practice makes perfect, so she'd have my mother to practice a song over and over again, until she could sing it so that it sounded just like it did on the record. Once she nailed it (which Momma always did, no matter which song it was), she'd move on to the next song.

My grandmother did not have a lot of extra money, but she spent what she could on the things she felt were most important for her daughter: to be independent, to have a career, and to be an entertainer (something she would have loved to do herself). She couldn't afford to buy all the latest fashions, but she was a good seamstress, so she would spend hours upon hours sewing dresses for my mom. This is another trait, self sacrifice, that Momma passed on to me. She went to great lengths for me growing up, above and beyond what could have been expected from any mother, and I strive to do the same for my own children.

* * *

In 1948, when Elvis was thirteen, his family moved to Memphis, Tennessee, drawing him one step closer to Momma (though neither of them knew it at the time). Momma's first step toward that path occurred two years later, in 1950, when she and her family attended a Sammy Kaye concert in Memphis. Sammy Kaye was a bandleader and songwriter during the Big Band Era; his tagline, "Swing and Sway with Sammy Kaye," was famous throughout the country. At one point during the show, Sammy asked for volunteers in the audience to become contestants in Sammy Kaye's "So You Want to Lead a Band." At Mamaw's prompting, my mother raised her hand and was selected for the contest; she then went on to become a finalist, and won the national competition on February 28, 1951. She was twelve years old. It was the first contest she'd ever won, and her first step in fulfilling Mamaw's dream for her.

By this time, Momma was already a member of the Juvenile Playhouse of Jackson, Tennessee; soon thereafter, she joined the Sub-Deb Club, an exclusive, "by invitation only" girls social organization. That same year, Mamaw entered Momma in her first talent contest, Perel & Lowenstein's "On Stage" show, held at the Malco Theatre in Jackson, Tennessee. Wearing a red evening dress Mamaw had made for her, she sang "If You Want Some Lovin'" by Teresa Brewer, and won the competition.

Two years later, around the time when Elvis graduated from Humes High School in Memphis, Momma won the lead role of Bertha, a blind girl, in *The Cricket on the Hearth*, a play performed by The Jackson Community Playhouse. She was just fourteen at the time. It was a difficult part, with a pivotal emotional scene, but she did an amazing job. The *Jackson Sun* not only said that "the first-nighters were spellbound [by] young Miss Anita Wood," but quoted a stage hand as saying that he was "in the wings when Anita was supposed to register tears," and that much to his surprise, "she produced the real thing."

Momma was not just another pretty face: she was smart, well liked by those who knew her, and very active in high school. Besides being in the National Honor Society, she was a cheerleader, a homecoming maiden, held an officer position in Kappa Chi Sorority, and won a writing competition sponsored by the Daughters of the American Revolution with a paper entitled "What Sets America Apart," which she read at graduation. She was also chosen Theta Kappa Omega Fraternity Sweetheart in 1954. In addition, she performed in many of her high school plays, including the lead in the play *Father Was a Housewife*, was in a number of variety shows throughout the community, including *A Little Bit of Everything*, sponsored by Sigma Alpha Epsilon, and the Pass In Review ceremony for the National Guardsmen of Jackson. She also did some modeling dinner shows for local department stores. (Meanwhile, during this time, Elvis made his first appearance on *The Louisiana Hayride*, as well as recorded "That's All Right" and "Blue Moon of Kentucky.")

Sixteen was a big year for Momma. She entered into the Mid-South Youth Talent Contest, where she sang "What a Dream" and won the local level, then won the regional level and, finally, the grand finale at the state competition. During this contest my mother and grandparents met Mrs. Patty, the executive assistant to the director of the Mid-South Fair. A nice woman who lived in Memphis, Mrs. Patty would soon play a significant role in Momma's life. So would one of the judges of the Mid-South Talent Content, Edwin Howard, a reporter for the *Memphis Press Scimitar* newspaper. Mr. Howard quickly became a fan of Momma's and wrote about her whenever opportunity arose (which of course, helped my mother become even more well-known with the general public).

Soon after winning this contest, Momma and Mamaw flew to New York. It was the first airplane ride for both of them, and the first of many plane trips that Momma had to make early in her career. Unlike most jet airliners of today, the passenger plane had only four propellers, so it was not exactly a smooth flight — and though air travel has improved considerably over the years, it left an indelible impression on my mother. Today you couldn't drag her on a plane for all the love or money in the world. I am not exaggerating, she simply will not fly.

Momma and her mother stayed in the Big Apple for several days. She was amazed by all the lights, concrete buildings, fast-moving cars, even faster-moving people and, of course, the skyscrapers. My grandmother loved everything about New York, but my mother was never crazy about it. She'd heard that New Yorkers were not very nice, and she told me that she did feel picked on somewhat, because of her Southern speech. I'd heard the same thing about New York, but when I had the opportunity to visit there some fifty-odd years later, I had the greatest time! (What can I say? In some ways, I must take after my grandmother.) While some people did walk around as if they couldn't be bothered, others were very friendly when I spoke to them. Everyone seemed to love my accent, and I loved listening to theirs. I was even proposed to a couple of times on the streets, which was really funny.

Meanwhile, all of Mamaw's efforts into my mother's future were beginning to pay off. While they were in New York, Momma auditioned with Paul Whiteman of the ABC television network (this would yield opportunities later). While she was still sixteen, she landed a job at WTJS, a local radio station in Jackson, where she hosted a teenage radio request show called *Antics of Anita*. My grandfather helped her come up with the name of the show, while Momma designed most of the program herself. She would take requests to play records, sing live in the studio for the audience, as well as sometimes interview teenagers on air. Momma's brothers, Jerry, Joe, and Andy, frequently dropped by during the show, as well as friends and fans. Sometimes she'd even dance with everyone while she was playing records on the air: she'd do the Bop, the Jitterbug, the Hucklebuck, the Bunny Hop, the Mashed Potato, the Twist, and all the other dances that were the rage when she was young. It was a very relaxed atmosphere (unlike that of talent contests, which is often tense and nerve-rattling), and Momma reveled in it.

Antics of Anita was so popular that Leslie Brooks, assistant manager of WTJS, once took Momma to a teenage programming seminar in Nashville. There, she met representatives from practically every major radio station in Tennessee, as well as network officials from New York. Momma talked to the assembled radiomen herself; they loved her program design so much that *Antics of Anita* became a prototype for most teenage shows put on the air thereafter.

Now, by this time, Elvis had released many records and was becoming quite popular among teenagers himself. And though Momma would play his records on her radio show, she herself, ironically enough, was not a big fan of his music. She much preferred listening to songs like "Unchained Melody" and "Dream Angel," as well as the music of Nat King Cole, the Drifters, and the Coasters.

On the home front, Momma's parents were very strict when it came to dating (not a surprise, from what you know about my grandfather), and kept her sheltered and naive. They would allow her to go on dates and to school dances, but they would not let her have a steady boyfriend. Truth be told, there was only one boy in high school that Momma would have liked to date steady. His name was Arthur Buehler, and he had a bad boy persona. So, of course, that meant he was off limits.

My grandfather's overprotective nature was particularly evident on the night when Momma had a date with a young man named Norris Taylor, a Delta Mu. She and Norris and some of their friends drove off together in Norris' car. Somehow my grandfather got wind that many of the kids had plans to go to a supper club that was also off-limits to Momma. W.A. didn't trust Norris, so he followed them. As it turned out, Norris and Momma dropped their friends off at the club and left, but not before they spotted my grandfather's car in the rearview mirror. (W.A. was a talented man, but he would have made a lousy detective.)

Naturally, Momma was furious and embarrassed and asked to be taken home right then. She was so hurt that her daddy didn't trust her, but all he said was, "Now, Anita, it's not that I don't trust you — I do trust you. I just don't trust that boy."

* * *

In 1955, when Momma turned seventeen, Elvis released "Heartbreak Hotel," which turned out to be his first Gold Record, as well as made his first movie, *Love Me Tender*. But it was a year of firsts for Momma as well. *Seventeen magazine* did an article on her, which meant more exposure for her radio show, as well as her social calendar. (As you can imagine, all of Momma's friends thought it was really cool to read about her in the magazine.)

After high school, Momma wanted to keep doing her radio show, so she spent one year at Lambeth College in her hometown of Jackson, Tennessee. There, she was a cheerleader, and had the lead in the play *The Barretts of Wimpole Street* (a role that required her to wear a hoop skirt, and learn how to maneuver in it). She also played Emily, the lead character in the play *Our Town*. If you have never seen *Our Town*, it is a fantastic play — and Momma must have done an excellent job, because Mamaw once told me that the audience was very emotional that night, and that some were still crying after the play was over. (When I was in college, I was the assistant director on the production of *Our Town* at the Vicksburg Little Theatre, where I lived. Funny, how life is so big and yet so small.)

The first time Momma actually saw Elvis was when he was on *The Ed Sullivan Show*. My grandmother was watching and called for my mom to come the living room: "Anita, come see this cute boy from Memphis."

Momma watched a little bit, agreed that he was cute... then went back to what she was doing.

Now, it's not like she didn't know who Elvis was — after all, she played his records all the time on her radio show. He just didn't tickle her fancy (at least, not yet). Besides, Momma has never been the type who easily becomes star-struck. "People are just people," she likes to say. "It doesn't matter what they do. Every person is just as important as the next. What really matters is how you treat people."

That's another bit of wisdom that she has passed on to my brothers and me. If I heard it once growing up, I heard it a thousand times: "Pretty is as pretty does!"

In 1956, when Momma was eighteen, she entered, at her parents' behest, the Miss Madison County Pageant. She sang "Too Young to Go Steady," causing photographers to start taking pictures and rolling their movie cameras. When asked by the judges what qualities she would look for in a husband, she replied, "I want my husband to be a Christian gentleman that would be loyal, honest, kind and understanding. I'd also want him, my husband, to be ambitious and keep striving for the top." She won the crown that night and advance to the Miss Tennessee Pageant, which she won swimsuit in the preliminaries, but placed first runner-up overall. Being only 5 foot 2, Momma felt her height was one factor that put her at a disadvantage. She clearly made an impression, however, because the next year, she was asked to perform at the Miss Tennessee Pageant as an entertainer.

For those of you who may not be familiar with pageants, the judges generally ask the contestants questions about topics that are hot at the time. So it's not surprising that Momma was asked about Elvis and rock 'n' roll.   When asked at the Miss Madison County Pageant for her thoughts on rock 'n' roll, Momma told the judges that she loved it, was afraid it was "on its way out," but wished that it would stay. Then, when one of the judges at the Miss Tennessee Pageant asked, "If Elvis Presley were to ask you for a date, what would be your reply," Momma said, "I don't think I'd care to date Elvis, although I do admire his music." Isn't life ironic!

Later that year, while Elvis was filming his second movie, *Loving You*, Momma continued to pursue her singing and acting career (which certainly pleased her parents). But though she loved to perform (and was certainly good at it), she never really liked the limelight. All she really wanted was a simple, normal life: to fall in love, get married and have a family of her own.

* * *

Top 10 Dance Party with Wink Martindale aired every Saturday afternoon on WHBQ-TV in Memphis. It was a very popular show at the time, especially among teens. Wink's female co-host, Susan Bancroft, was leaving the program, and he was looking for her replacement. More than 700 people vied for the job, including my mom. She doesn't remember much about the audition, except that it was just before her nineteenth birthday, and she sat on a stool and talked about Coca Cola. (Coca Cola was a sponsor of the show, so I'm sure that it didn't hurt to let them know how much she loved the product.) In any event, Wink suggested to WHBQ general manager Bill Grumbles and program director Mark Forrester that the station hire Momma as Susie's replacement. "I totally enjoyed working with Anita," Wink recalled. "We were always good friends."

Momma knew this was a great opportunity, but because she'd never been away from home before, it was also a little scary. So Mamaw called Mrs. Patty, the woman they'd met a few years before, at the Mid-South Talent Contest. Turns out, she had a large house in Memphis, near the Memphian Theatre, and told my grandmother that she would love for Momma to come live with her. She was a widow and already had her brother, his wife and another girl named Mamie Walker living with her, so for Momma it would be like having a surrogate family. Mrs. Patty treated her like a daughter, and made her feel secure. Momma liked her very much.

Momma first appeared on *Top 10 Dance Party* on May 25, 1957. She played music, interviewed kids, danced some, and did commercials, much as she did on her radio show. But because this was television, she was now seen as well as heard. The job was a lot of fun and Momma loved every minute of it. She didn't feel under pressure there (which was the main thing she hated about the entertainment business), so this was clearly a good fit. (In the meantime, she left her radio show in the good hands of her brother Jerry, who changed the name to *Jiving with Jerry*.)

Anita with her family: Dorothy (her mother),
Andy, Joe, and Jerry (her brothers)
(from the collection of Anita Wood)

Anita at age ten or eleven

Anita won Sammy Kaye's "So You Want to Lead a Band"
contest when she was twelve years old
(both photos from the collection of Anita Wood)

Autographed picture of Anita as a teen. (Courtesy of James V Roy)

Antics of Anita, July 18, 1955. *(Courtesy of Memphis Press-Scimitar Morgue Files/Special Collections, University of Memphis Libraries)*

Anita at age sixteen when she hosted her own radio show, *Antics of Anita*, and won the Mid-South Fair Talent Contest *(Coutesy of Memphis Press-Scimitar)*

High school graduation picture, 1956
(from the collection of Anita Wood)

L.H. Dille from the Mid-South Fair presents Anita with corsage before she leaves for her trip to New York, December 13, 1954. *(Courtesy of Memphis Press-Scimitar Morgue Files/Special Collections, University of Memphis Libraries)*

Preparing for the Miss Tennessee Pageant. Anita was named first runner-up and selected "Miss Congeniality." *(from the collection of Anita Wood)*

Chapter 2

The Infamous First Date

One Saturday in the summer of 1957, after finishing the taping of *Top 10 Dance Party*, Momma received a phone call at the station. On the line was Lamar Fike, a member of Elvis Presley's ever-present entourage. "Elvis saw you on the show today. He'd like to take you out tonight."

Now, most girls would've screamed with excitement at the thought of Elvis Presley asking them out. But by now, you know that Momma was not like most girls. "I'm sorry," she told Lamar, "but I already have a date tonight."

Needless to say, Elvis and his minions were not used to being told no. "Girl, have you lost your mind? *Elvis Presley is asking you out*," Lamar said. "Are you telling me you won't break a date to go out with Elvis Presley?!??"

Momma paused for a moment. "Well, it's not that I don't want to, Mr. Fike — I do. But let's put it on the flip side. If I had a date with Elvis, and canceled it to go out with someone else, I reckon he wouldn't appreciate that one bit. Well, I just couldn't do that to anyone, not even for Elvis."

Lamar Fike would have none of it. "Girl, you are crazy," he said as he angrily hung up.

Bear in mind, Momma knew who she was talking to, and that there was a very good chance that she would never hear from Elvis Presley again. But she also believed in treating others the way she would like to be treated — and hard though it was, this was one of those times when she knew she had to walk the walk.

Still, it flattered her to know that Elvis wanted to go out with her. She immediately called her mother, who told her not to worry: "Elvis will call you back."

Momma wasn't so sure, however — and though she kept her date that night (with a boy named Jimmy Omar), her mind was clearly elsewhere. She tried her best not to show it and, of course, she never told Jimmy about the phone call. But every time she heard an Elvis song on the radio that night, she kept thinking about what might have been. Poor Jimmy, he never really stood a chance!

* * *

About a week later, as my grandmother predicted, Lamar called Momma again at the station: "Elvis would like to take you out tonight. Are you available?" (I've always wondered why Elvis didn't call Momma himself, but I guess by that point, he had become accustomed to having someone else do things for him. Besides, no guy likes to be turned down, not even Elvis Presley.)

Well, wouldn't you know, Momma was free that night, and so she said yes. Needless to say, she was walking tall and very excited the rest of the day.

When Momma got home, she immediately told Mrs. Patty that she was going out with Elvis. But to her surprise, Mrs. Patty insisted that when he arrived, he would have to come to the door himself and pick her up, like a proper gentleman. Mrs. Patty was as big an Elvis fan as they come, but she didn't like it that he didn't call Momma himself. Like any good mother (or in this case, surrogate mother), she wanted a chance to make sure Elvis was a nice boy and that he'd treat Momma with respect.

I realize that some of you might think Mrs. Patty was being silly — after all, this was Elvis Presley. But it was not uncommon back then for parents to expect a boy to ask for their blessing before taking their daughter out on a date. We've let this practice go by the wayside in today's culture, and I think we've suffered for it. Today, girls and guys just meet up, without the parents having a chance to talk to the young man and make sure he will protect, respect, and bring his date home safely. It shows little faith in our boys, and leaves our girls exposed and unprotected. That's just my opinion, as a mother of two boys and two girls.

* * *

That night, around eight o'clock, Momma stood by the front window, peering outside every so often (like most girls do, when they're waiting for a date). She wore a pink princess-style dress, which Mamaw had sewn for her, with lots of crinoline slips underneath that made her skirt stand out, and her waist seem even smaller — which, considering Momma had only a 22-inch waist to begin with, was not something she needed help with! In any event, she felt her heart racing when she suddenly saw a big, long, shiny black Cadillac limousine pull up in front of Mrs. Patty's house. In it, of course, was Elvis and his entourage.

As Momma gathered her purse, Mrs. Patty answered the door — only to find George Klein standing on the front step. George worked with Momma at the TV station; no doubt Elvis had asked him to greet her at the door in order to make her feel comfortable. Except that Mrs. Patty would have none of that.

"Good evening," said George. "I'm here to pick up Anita."

"I'm sorry," said Mrs. Patty. "If Elvis wants to see her, then he'll have to come to the door himself and pick her up himself."

George stood there for a moment looking perplexed before heading back to the limousine. I can only imagine what Elvis must have thought when he learned what Mrs. Patty had said. But nonetheless, he got out of the car, and walked back to the house with George.

When Momma first laid eyes on Elvis, she was stunned by his overwhelming good looks. Despite the warm weather, he wore a long-sleeved, red velvet blousy shirt (much like the one he wore in the movie *Loving You*, which he had just finished filming), with black trousers and a black motorcycle hat. As handsome as he was on television, he looked even better in person.

Elvis and George greeted Mrs. Patty. George introduced Elvis to Momma, and they all chatted a bit in the living room. Then Mrs. Patty said to Elvis, "Now, you have her back at a reasonable hour."

"Oh, yes, I will, ma'am," said Elvis to Mrs. Patty. "It's been so nice to meet you." He said it with all his Southern charm, and he sounded completely sincere.

Elvis opened the door to the front seat for Momma, then walked around to the driver's side. As she waited, she heard some giggling in the back. That's when she realized there were four other guys besides George sitting in the back. Naturally, she thought this was strange, but at least she recognized a few of them.

George sat next to Cliff Gleaves, who was from Momma's hometown of Jackson, Tennessee. He was a good bit older than Momma, but she knew him, as well as his little brother. Also in the back was Lamar Fike, of course, as well as Lewis Harris, a cameraman at Momma's station. Lewis was a good friend of Alan Fortas, who was also seated in the back. Momma didn't know Alan yet, but they would become very good friends in the future.

Momma sat as close as she could to the door, as any respectable girl would do (especially on a first date). She'd never been in a limousine before, so she was excited and nervous at the same time. She'd always imagined that one usually rides in the back of a limousine, not the front. Looking back, I suppose you might say this was her first indication that life with Elvis would be anything but usual.

Elvis drove around Memphis, talking to Momma some while also kidding around with the guys. He asked how she liked doing "that TV show," and the other sort of small-talk questions one asks a girl on a first date. What Momma remembers most about that part of the evening is the mischievous twinkle in his eyes whenever he smiled at her, and how polite and funny he was. That, and how whenever Elvis spoke to her, he made her feel like they were the only two people in the car.

After a while, Elvis noticed how far apart Momma was sitting from him. "You're mighty far away over there," he said. "You trying to knock the door out or something?"

"No," said Momma.

"Well, scoot on over here then," he said, patting the seat next to him.

Slowly, tentatively, Momma slid over about three inches.

Elvis and the guys couldn't help but laugh; they thought that was hilarious. Even Momma thought it was funny. But she didn't move another inch.

Meanwhile, the boys in the back kept howling with laughter. "Don't you know who you're on a date with? *This is Elvis Presley!*"

Then again, by this time I'm sure Elvis was figuring out that the girl sitting next to him was no ordinary date, either.

* * *

Elvis pulled into a Krystal restaurant, then sent Lamar inside to buy some hamburgers. Needless to say, going to a fast-food place was not exactly what Momma had in mind.

Elvis asked her what she wanted. "I'll just have a Coke please," she said politely.

"Are you sure?" he asked. "He's gonna get a couple dozen burgers."

"That's okay," she said. The truth is, she didn't like Krystal hamburgers because she doesn't like onions. But she didn't want him to special-order anything, either.

Elvis drove silently, while the rest of the boys wolfed down hamburgers. Then he looked into Momma's eyes and asked, "Would you like to come out and see Graceland?" He had just purchased it at the time and was understandably proud.

Momma hesitated to answer; after all, she'd never been to a man's house before. Then she reminded herself that, besides being the most handsome man she'd ever met, Elvis had already made quite a good impression on her. She felt comfortable with him, especially because he'd made a point of bringing along some people that she already knew. Plus Momma knew that Elvis' parents lived with him at Graceland, so it would probably be okay.

"Sure," she said. "I'd love to."

* * *

Some fans were gathered at the gate when they arrived at Graceland. As Elvis drove past them, he invited them, as he always did, to come up to the house. Momma didn't know what to make of that, but that was part of what made Elvis unique. He was always incredibly generous to his fans, and treated them thoughtfully. That's another aspect of that time that is unfortunately lost today. Celebrities today, for reasons of safety, simply cannot afford to do that.

Elvis pulled up in front of the house and talked to the fans while everyone else piled out of the car. Then, like a perfect gentleman, he opened the front door for Momma, put his arm around her shoulders, and started showing her around Graceland. It was the first time that he had touched her, and she thought that it was very nice — except he wouldn't take off his motorcycle hat! Her brothers had been taught to always remove their hats once they're inside. But Elvis kept his hat on the entire night. Momma thought that was very odd.

My mom had never seen anything quite like Graceland: It was larger than life in every possible way, and yet beautiful just the same. She noticed the dining room with the antique cabinet and the long dining room table. There were also teddy bears all over the place, because Elvis had just released "Teddy Bear" only a few weeks before.

He picked up a pink and black teddy bear and handed it to Momma. "I'd like you to have this," he said.

"Thank you," she said. "That's very sweet."

The living room, which was on the right, had a beautiful fireplace surrounded by humongous mirrors. There was also a huge sectional couch, a large coffee table, and lots of gold, floral and red chairs. A back staircase came from upstairs, leading straight to the kitchen, which had a big bar rounded off on the end. Alberta, the Presley's housekeeper and cook, was tidying up, while some of the guys were seated at the bar. As Elvis introduced Alberta, Momma could see her room through an open door off the kitchen.

As Elvis continue to show Momma around, he must have been looking her over, because he kept commenting on how petite she was: "Just look at you, you are so little. Your feet are simply tiny!" In fact, it was that very night that he gave her the nickname "Little." She really was tiny all over: Momma was small boned, and wore a size 5 in shoes.

Eventually they stopped by his parents' room on the main floor. His mother and father were watching television. Elvis kissed his mom on the cheek and gave her a big hug. "I want you both to meet Anita," he said. "She's on that television dance show."

"I've seen you on that show," said Mr. Presley. "You do a mighty fine job."

Mrs. Presley took Momma by the hand and showed her around the room. There were French doors off the side, leading toward the swimming pool outside. Inside, there was a king size bed, a couple of recliners, the television set, and a huge walk-in closet filled with dresses.

Atop the dresser were some photos of Elvis from when he was a little boy. Mrs. Presley picked up a few and showed them to Momma. She was very proud of her little boy, and Momma thought he looked adorable.

Meanwhile, Elvis stood in the back of the room, watching television with his father. "Isn't she little, Sattinin!" he suddenly exclaimed. (Sattinin was a nickname that Elvis sometimes called his mother.)

Then Elvis and his mother started gritting their teeth and talking "baby talk," saying things to each other like "I could just pinch your yittle nose!" Momma had never heard or seen anything like it before — and for a moment, she wondered just what kind of person Elvis was.

She quickly realized, however, this was one of the ways in which Elvis showed affection to the people who were close to him. Most boys she knew wouldn't dare show their feelings towards their parents, especially in front of a date. But it was apparent that Elvis loved his parents very much, and didn't mind showing it. Momma could appreciate that, because she was close to her family, too (even without the baby talk).

It wouldn't be long before Elvis started talking to Momma that way, too. As she grew to love and understand this language, he would say things to her like "yuv" (instead of love), "butch" (instead of milk), "yittle" (little), "sooties" (feet), "toophies" (teeth), as well as "yittle us" and "him yuvs her."

* * *

Graceland is a palatial, three-story house, and Elvis was determined to show Momma every room before their date was over. After finishing the tour of the main floor, Elvis and Momma joined some of the guests in the music room. There was a white and gold baby grand piano inside, and as Elvis sat down to play, he invited Momma to join him on the piano bench. Not only was she happy to oblige, she felt her heart leap just a little. Here he was, the most handsome man in the world, and she was sitting right next to him.

Momma had no idea that Elvis could play the piano. He actually chorded the music by ear (which he later taught her to do). Everyone else's eyes were on Elvis, yet once again he made Momma feel like she was the only person in the room.

Then Elvis invited Momma, and the rest of his entourage, to join him downstairs. The first thing she noticed at the bottom of the stairs was a Pepsi soda fountain machine with crushed ice on a recessed bar. It looked just like the kind you'd see at a fast food place, and had everything you'd need to fix a soft drink.

On the left side of this landing was a room with a tan leather sectional couch and a couple of large television sets. Elvis could watch two shows at once, if he wanted to. Along the wall to the left of the TV sets hung frames of Elvis' gold records and other assorted awards. On the right side of the landing was the billiards room, which boasted a pretty and unusual ceiling, a very nice pool table and pool stick rack, plus tables and chairs all around.

Momma sat and watched as Elvis played pool with the guys. He never left her unattended for long, though, because he constantly came over to ask, "Are you okay, Little?" or "Do you need anything?" Sometimes he'd kiss her on the cheek, as if they'd known each other for a long time. He also explained what they were doing, which Momma appreciated because she knew nothing about the game of pool. "You try to get that black ball in last, Little," she remembers him saying.

As the night went on, Momma became more and more enchanted by Elvis: she liked the way he moved, the way he laughed, his sense of humor, the way he treated people and, of course, the way he treated her. Somehow, he made her feel as she'd known him all of her life.

* * *

After a while, Elvis said, "I want you to meet my grandma and also see my office and my room." Momma followed him upstairs while the others continued to shoot pool.

Elvis' grandmother was sitting in a rocking chair, watching television. Her room had a king size bed and regular bedroom furniture. She was a tall woman, fairly thin but big boned, with grey hair that was pulled back in a bun at her neck. She had a sweet gum twig about the size of a match sticking out of her mouth, plus she was chewing snuff. Momma noticed she didn't have any teeth.

"Dodger, this is Anita," Elvis said. By now it was apparent to Momma that Elvis liked nicknames, and "Dodger" was his name for his grandma.

"How do you do," smiled Dodger as she gave her a big hug. They visited for a while before Elvis showed Momma the rest of the house, including a room across the hall, where some of the guys stayed from time to time.

Then Elvis led Momma through big double doors to show her his office. There was a large desk, along with some chairs, a record player, and a state-of-the-art sound system. The furnishings were extravagant and flamboyant, very much in character with Elvis, while the predominant color in the room was orange red.

Elvis sat behind his desk and played a demo so that Momma could hear his sound system. Then he invited her to his room. That was the only room in the house she hadn't seen — and as you might imagine, she was a little nervous. Other than her brothers' room, she had never been in a man's bedroom before.

There was a little walkway between his office and bedroom. When they entered the bedroom, Elvis turned on the lights because it was very dark inside (no outside light could get in). There were navy blue walls, thick navy blue drapes, and a navy blue spread on a gigantic bed that seemed to be much, much bigger than a king size. Mirrors were all over the place, while both sides of the hall had closets that were packed with clothes. One was a pants closet, while the other had shirts and jackets. She doesn't think that he ever wore the same thing twice.

He took her past the closets, down the hallway and into his bathroom, which had a baby blue sink and baby blue bathroom fixtures. The walls were white with light blue trimmed mirrors everywhere, while the carpet was a plush, thick baby blue furry design that your feet just sank into.

As Momma turned to leave the bathroom, Elvis grabbed her around her waist and kissed her right on the mouth. Now, back in those days, you just didn't kiss a girl on a first date, so naturally, Momma was surprised — and yet, at the same time, she liked it! In her mind, she thought if Elvis was kissing her like that, he must like her in the same way that she was beginning to like him.

Then he walked her over to the end of his bed, sat her down, and began kissing her some more. Elvis was such a good kisser, it was hard not to get lost in the moment. But when his hands started moving across her body, Momma said, "Oh, no, no, I don't feel comfortable with this. I need to go home."

Elvis hadn't expected that at all — but to his credit he stopped immediately and said, "Okay." Still, from the wounded puppy dog look on his face, it was clear that he was not used to being rejected.

"Don't you like me, Little?" he finally asked.

Momma didn't know what to say other than to tell the truth. "Yes, I like you, Elvis... but this is our first date."

Elvis sat there looking confused for a moment before finally saying, "Okay." Then he helped Momma gather her things and decided to take her home.

By the time they pulled up in front of Mrs. Patty's house, it was almost two in the morning, which was not exactly a "reasonable hour," as Elvis had promised (though perhaps, for him, it was). Fortunately for Momma, Mrs. Patty was sound asleep, so any explanations would have to wait till the next day.

Elvis got out of the limousine, opened the door, and walked Momma to the front porch. When they got to the front door, he gave her such a big hug, they almost fell off the porch! Then he put his hand on Momma's face and neck and gently kissed her again.

"I told you, I don't usually kiss boys on a first date," she said breathlessly.

Elvis laughed. "Oh, you yittle thing, you," he said in baby talk.

Finally, it was time to go inside. "I enjoyed myself and had a good time," she said. "Good night."

"I'll call you later," said Elvis. Then he walked back to the car and drove off.

She wasn't sure if he would ask her out again. Nor was she sure if it would be the best thing to go out with him again, even if he did ask. And yet her heart longed to see him again.

Chapter 3

Falling in Love

Momma had a hard time sleeping that night. All she could do was think of Elvis — how handsome he was, how attentive and affectionate, his sense of humor and, of course, the way she felt all over whenever he held and kissed her. He was so gentle, so playful, and oh, so intoxicating. The evening was bizarre at times, for sure, but overall it was simply magical.

As she lay in bed, Momma realized just how much she liked Elvis. And yet when she thought about what happened in his bedroom, she also had her worries. She knew he was testing the waters, so to speak, just like any man would. But she'd never let anyone else go as far as he did that night (especially on a first date), and she wanted to do what was right.

Still, Elvis didn't seem too put out when she told him to stop, and Momma knew that was a good thing. But would he call her again?

Momma had stopped other boys' advances before without caring whether she heard from them again. But with Elvis, it was different. She wanted him to call her more than anything in the world.

The next morning, as you can imagine, Mrs. Patty was eager to hear all the details. Except for the bedroom scene, of course, Momma told her pretty much everything.

Mrs. Patty was none too pleased about Elvis keeping Momma out so late. But she cut him slack once she learned about his "backward schedule," as Momma put it. Because Elvis was so famous, he couldn't go out in public during the daytime, like anyone else — otherwise, he'd be mobbed. That's why he kept such late hours.

Momma also explained that Elvis' parents and grandmother lived with him at Graceland, plus he always had a bunch of people around, "so it wasn't like I was in a man's house all by myself." Mrs. Patty liked hearing that; otherwise, being that she was, in effect, Momma's guardian at the time (and putting aside how much she personally loved Elvis' music), she would have found it unacceptable for a young girl to go to a young man's house on a first date. Even if he was Elvis Presley.

Meanwhile, Momma spent the next few hours eagerly waiting for the phone to ring (forgetting, of course, that given his "backward schedule," Elvis slept during the daytime hours). Finally, later that afternoon, the phone rang at Mrs. Patty's house — and this time, it was Elvis himself: "Hey, Little, you wanna drive on out to the house?"

"Me, drive out there?" Momma asked.

31

Obviously, this is not what she was expecting. But if the previous night had taught Momma anything, it was that dating Elvis would never be normal. "Sure... I can do that," she said. "When would you like me to come over?"

"How 'bout now?" said Elvis. "I thought we'd have breakfast and spend the day together."

That was Lesson No. 2 for Momma. Elvis did not make plans ahead of time; everything was spur of the moment. So she freshened up as fast as she could and hurried out the door, smiling all the way.

* * *

Momma was driving an old, light green Ford at the time, a graduation present from her grandparents that helped her get around town. She rode up to the gate at Graceland, pulled around to the back of the house and entered through the kitchen. Elvis greeted her with a kiss before bringing her into the dining room. He sat at the head of the table, with the rest of the guys seated around him. He motioned to the empty chair next to him empty and invited Momma to sit down. He ate lots and lots of extra crisp bacon — in fact, Momma remembers that if the bacon wasn't crisp enough, he would send it back to the kitchen and ask Alberta to cook it some more. He also had two fried eggs that were broken and almost burnt, sliced tomatoes, and fresh-baked Colonial clover rolls.

That evening, they stayed home and watched television, shot some pool, and sat at the piano and sang. After dinner, Elvis invited the fans from the gate to come up to the house. He liked to have a good time, and always kept it festive at night.

At some point while they were playing pool, Elvis felt hungry, so he asked Momma to fix him a Pepsi and one of his favorite sandwiches: peanut butter and mashed banana on white bread. Momma had never heard of this before, so he told her how to fix it. "You put some peanut butter in a bowl and mash the banana into it with a fork," he said. "That's the way I like it."

Well, that's different, Momma thought.

My grandmother taught Momma a great many things, but cooking was not one of them — Mamaw didn't like anyone else around whenever she made meals. So Momma was not exactly at home in the kitchen. Nonetheless, she puttered around till she found everything she needed, and did the best she could. While making Elvis' sandwich, she made a half-one for herself so she could try it. To her surprise, she thought it tasted pretty good! (Years later, when I was a little girl, Momma showed me how to make that sandwich, so I ate them all the time.)

Momma learned very quickly that Elvis had a peculiar appetite. He didn't like fish at all, and he didn't eat much meat. But he did like things like sauerkraut, greens, purple hull peas, tomatoes, country fried potatoes (sliced real thin and cooked very crisp), colonial rolls, and crisp, crisp bacon. In fact, he liked just about everything well done — and as it happens, so does Momma. When I was growing up, we used to tease her that whenever she burnt something, she must've done it on purpose, because that's the way she liked it.

* * *

One day Momma's parents and brothers came to visit her at Mrs. Patty's house, and while they were there Elvis dropped by to meet them. He charmed them all, and while they may have been star-struck to some extent, they also came away totally impressed with how personable and nice he was. Elvis was nothing if not effervescent: he could light up a room just by walking in it, and he had a knack for putting people at ease and making them feel good about themselves. That's what made him so special.

Now that Elvis had met the approval of Momma's family, the question was, were they going steady, or just dating. Momma wasn't sure herself at that point, but she would soon find out. In fact, it wasn't long after meeting his parents that Elvis started calling Momma almost every night and invited her to come by Graceland.

Sometimes he would even ride out to Mrs. Patty's house himself — usually on his motorcycle, and always wearing a motorcycle hat. He and Momma would stand and talk in front of the house until the neighbors started coming outside to watch (and, almost always, take pictures). One time, a neighbor gave Momma one of these photos. Elvis was standing in front of his motorcycle, with his cap on and his hands on his hips, while she stood in front of him, wearing high heels and a tight sailor dress.

Momma loved that photo, because it was taken by a neighbor, not the press. She kept it in her wallet for years, until one day in the 1970s someone stole it from her. No money was taken from the wallet, mind you — just the photograph! Whoever took it had to be someone close enough to Momma to know that she carried that picture with her. As special as that photo was to her, that hurt her even more.

One day, Elvis invited Momma to ride with him on his motorcycle. "Oh, no, I don't think I want to," she said. "I'm afraid of motorcycles."

"You ever been on one before?" asked Elvis.

"No," said Momma, with a little hesitation.

"Then how do you know you're afraid of them?" He said it with such charm that she could not help but smile.

"Come on, Little, it'll be fun," Elvis continued. "You'll love it, and I promise, I will be very careful. You will not get hurt. Come on."

Only because it was Elvis, Momma got on that motorcycle behind him and wrapped her arms tightly around his waist. Sure enough, she grew to like riding with him, because of the freedom he felt — and the closeness she felt experiencing that freedom with him.

Riding the motorcycle was an escape for Elvis. As much as he liked having all the guys around, sometimes he wanted to be by himself, or just be with my mom. Riding his motorcycle made him feel like he was riding the wind, and that he had total control.

Sometimes Elvis would ride around with Momma in the old paneled truck that he used to drive when he worked for the electric company, before he became famous. He would drive her around Lauderdale Courts and show her where he used to live, where he went to school, and other places from his past.

Elvis told Momma how close he was to his mom and his dad. "Growing up was hard for me, when we came to Memphis," he said. "We didn't have any money, so we had to live in Lauderdale Courts, which is a place for poor people to live." He told Momma that people made fun of him when he went to Humes High School, because he had long hair and didn't look or act like anyone else. "The football boys were distant," he said, "and made fun of me the most."

He talked about meeting George Klein in high school, and how they became close friends. He spoke of the time when he won a talent contest at the school, and how that helped him become well known. (Elvis liked winning that contest because it was something he'd done for himself.) He also told Momma that he had learned to play the guitar in Tupelo, Mississippi, with some of the black people there that he considered his friends. They would play around, chording on the guitar, as well as play the blues.

"My momma always encouraged me because she thought I could really sing," Elvis said. "She just loved to hear me sing."

Elvis also told Momma the story about the first record he ever made, "My Happiness." His mother, Gladys, loved that song, so he walked into Sam Phillips Studio one day and recorded it for her birthday. Of course, Elvis had no idea how much his life would change soon long after making that record. All he knew was that it was an act of love that he did for his momma, and she thought it was especially sweet.

My mother loved riding around Elvis, partly because she was new to Memphis and still learning her way around town. (Talk about your own personal tour guide!) But mostly she cherishes those moments because it was just of the two of them together.

Of course, whenever they came to a red light or stop sign, people would recognize them and say, "Hey, look, there's Elvis and Anita!" Some fans would try to talk to Elvis; sometimes he would say, "Hey, how are you doing," but most times he was anxious for the light to change so that he could take off. As much as he loved mingling with his fans at Graceland, Elvis did not encourage much conversation during the day, and especially in an uncontrolled environment, because of the frenzy it could cause.

* * *

The more Momma got to know Elvis, the more he got to know her. They talked about each other's childhood, and also what they believed in.

One day Momma asked Elvis if he was saved. For those of you who may not know this expression, it is used often in the South, and asks the question, do you believe in Jesus Christ as God's only Son, that died for your sins and rose again on the third day. Have you repented of your sins and do you accept Jesus as your Savior. By turning from your sins and accepting Jesus as your Lord and Savior, you are therefore saved from the penalty of your sins, which is eternal separation from God in a place of great torment called Hell.

It brought great joy to my mother's heart when Elvis told her, "Yes, Little, I am saved," and that he had attended the Assembly of God church while he was growing up. Momma said that she was raised as a Baptist and had never heard of his church before. But as long as Elvis was a Christian, that was all right with her.

Music was another bond that brought them both together. Elvis loved gospel music, and he often took Momma to gospel quartet concerts at the Memphis Coliseum. They would sit backstage, and sometimes Elvis would even go out on stage and perform songs with them. He knew all the songs by heart, and his favorite vocal part was bass. He loved sitting backstage with the musicians learning the bass part.

Elvis liked that Momma had been a disc jockey and was very knowledgeable about music. He often asked her to sing for him whenever they sat at the piano. It was also during this time that he taught Momma how to chord songs. He would say, "It's like this, Little: When you sing a song, you chord, C, D, E, F, with the song." Sometimes, while Elvis was off doing something else, she would sit at the piano in the music room and practice what he had taught her.

Now you want to hear something strange? Whenever he and Momma sat at the piano, Elvis rarely played or sang one of his own songs. Instead, he would sing songs from other artists, or ask Momma to sing while he joined in with a harmony part. He would say, "Little, do it this way," and then they would sing together. Some of their favorite songs that they sang together included "You Win Again," "Who's Sorry Now," "Unchained Melody" and "I Can't Help It If I'm Still in Love with You."

* * *

One of their favorite places to go was Chenault's, a restaurant in Memphis that had a private room in the back, complete with its own entrance. Elvis liked Chenault's because of the privacy, plus the owners were so very nice and accommodating. The jukebox, of course, had several of Elvis's records (and later, after Momma began recording, some of her records as well). Knowing that Elvis often ate in the back room, the customers at Chenault's would play his songs (and, later, Momma's songs) to let them know that there were fans out front.

Elvis always got a kick out of that. "Listen, Little, there you are," he would say to my mother. "They're playing your song."

The first time they went to Chenault's, Momma discovered another one of Elvis' unusual eating habits. Sitting at the head of the table, with Momma seated to his right, he decided he wanted a hamburger.

Now, Chenault's was sort of a high end restaurant — not exactly a burger joint. But whatever Elvis wanted, Chenault's was glad to provide. So he ordered a plate of fried, crisp, crisp bacon, a plate of sliced tomatoes, and a hamburger bun. Then he proceeded to make his own burger, with everything *except* the hamburger patty!

Needless to say, Momma had never seen anything like that before. But that was Elvis. He liked simple things to eat, and simple food is what he ordered. And if the bacon was not crisp enough to his liking, he wouldn't hesitate to send it back to the kitchen until it was done just right, the way he liked it at home.

Still, sometimes I'd wonder why Elvis would go to the trouble of taking Momma out to eat when all he'd order was the same thing that he could have Alberta make him at home. The answer, Momma said, was simple: "It was something to do, and we always had fun. We all got to talk and laugh together in one room, plus the excitement of the fans in the next room playing his music made it that much more fun."

Life was certainly good back then, and my mother remembers many such moments that were filled with laughter. Everything was going Elvis' way, and everyone got to share in what was really the making of a legend.

* * *

Elvis also liked to take Momma to the movies. During the daytime, they would sneak into the balcony of the Malco Theater (the man who ran it was a friend of Elvis' family), and watch three movies in a row. Much to Momma's chagrin, however, they were usually Westerns. Momma was never a big fan of Westerns, although she did like John Wayne. But if Elvis wanted to see a Western, then that's what she would do, because it meant spending time together. Sometimes he would hold her hand during the movie or put his arm around her shoulder; sometimes he'd give her a peck on the check, or just pet her like a baby, very loving and sweet. (Sometimes, however, he'd talk to the boys during the movie — but he'd always do it quietly, because he knew there were people downstairs.)

One day Elvis thought, "Wouldn't it be great, Little, if I had my own private movie theater? We could go whenever we wanted, and talk whenever we wanted, and not worry about anyone else."

Well, as it happened, the man who ran the Malco Theater also knew the owner of the Memphian Theater; he talked the Memphian into renting the theater out after hours, just for Elvis and his friends. Sometimes, as they left Graceland to drive their way to the theater, Elvis would stop at the gate and invite the fans that were waiting there to go to the movies with them. (He would hand out a bunch of red tickets that the theater had given him. In fact, Momma still has a stack of Memphian tickets among her mementos.)

Momma was glad Elvis was able to rent the theater. She never did like sneaking in the back way, and now they could go in through the foyer, like everyone else. Elvis would walk about halfway down the aisle and sit right in the middle of the row, with Momma sitting beside him. No one else ever sat next to him — they might sit a few seats over, or maybe behind him, but *never* in front of him.

I told you that Elvis liked Westerns. He also liked John Wayne movies, Marlon Brando movies, sad movies, happy movies, and funny movies. They were always first-run movies, and always good ones.

One night, while they were watching *Psycho*, Elvis turned to Momma and said, "Hey, Little, you look just like Janet Leigh. Just look at her eyes."
Another movie they watched together was *Splendor in the Grass*, with Natalie Wood. Momma remembers that she and Elvis both cried that night.

Most nights, she and Elvis would watch two or three movies in a row. Momma was usually tired by the time the last one was over, but Elvis, being a night owl, would still be wide awake, and almost always hungry. So they would stop by Chenault's or somewhere else for a bite to eat on the way home.

One night, one of the fans who were waiting at the gate was my daddy, Johnny Brewer. He was playing football at the time at Ole Miss, in Oxford, Mississippi, which is just an hour outside of Memphis. Daddy and a friend had decided to drive up to Graceland, hoping that Elvis would invite them up to the house. Instead Elvis invited them to join Momma and him at the movies.

Daddy and his friend were standing in the lobby when Elvis and Momma arrived. That was the first time Daddy would ever lay his eyes on her, and he thought she was one of the most beautiful women he had ever seen.

Of course, Momma didn't pay attention to him, because her eyes were glued on Elvis. Being a good-looking man himself, Daddy wasn't used to that — he had dated quite a few beauties from Ole Miss, including two Miss Americas.

But as Momma told him many years later, "You didn't look at anyone else when you were with Elvis, because he was extremely possessive."

Later that night Daddy and Elvis met each other while they were in the men's room. Elvis knew who he was; he liked football, and had seen my father play at Ole Miss. At one point, while they were still in the restroom, one of the guys from Elvis' entourage (Daddy didn't remember who) tried to bum some money off Elvis and wouldn't leave them alone until he got it. That irritated Elvis, and Daddy remembered him muttering something like "Damn leech." That was about the extent of their conversation.

* * *

When *Loving You* premiered in Memphis in July 1957, Elvis took Momma, his parents, and some of the guys to a special midnight screening. It was the first time Momma and Elvis watched one of his movies together, and she thought it was surreal to be sitting beside him, along with his folks, while also seeing him on the big screen. Throughout the picture Elvis would say things like "See how I did that, Little?" or "Did you like that, Momma?" He also pointed out a lot of things that were happening behind the scenes. It was a really good movie; Elvis seemed pleased with his performance, and his parents were very proud of him.

One afternoon, when the guys were itching for something to do, Elvis said, "Come on, let's all take a ride." So he, Momma, and three of the guys climbed into his purple convertible and headed south. They ended up in Tupelo. There, Elvis showed Momma where he used to live and walk and go to school. He talked about the troubles he had in school, the problems he had as a boy, and how he became so close to his mother when his dad had gone to prison.

Momma had never seen poverty like that first hand, but Elvis really wanted her, and his friends, to understand where he came from, what had happened to him, and how much he had to overcome. He was not ashamed of his less fortunate roots; rather, he was very proud of the fact that he had achieved so much, from having started with nothing at all. Just as important, even though his circumstances had changed dramatically, he was still the same person. He was living proof that dreams do come true.

* * *

Even though Momma had never had a steady boyfriend before Elvis, and was still very green when it came to relationships, she knew that something special was going on between them. When there's real chemistry, you just know it. So it wasn't a surprise when one night, after seeing each other almost every day for about a month or so, Elvis said out loud to Momma what she herself had been feeling inside her heart.

Looking back, it was pretty clear that he wanted this night to be special, because instead of asking Momma to drive out to Graceland, Elvis picked her up himself at Mrs. Patty's house. At the end of the evening, he walked her to the front porch and kissed her goodnight. Then, just as Momma was about open to the door, Elvis stopped her and said, "Little, wait a minute, I think I'm falling in love with you."

Momma turned around and kissed him again. She was thrilled beyond belief to know that he felt that way about her — after all, he'd never even "gotten to first base" with her (not that he didn't try), and she was afraid that he might be confused over how she really felt about him. Now that she knew that he loved her, whatever lingering doubts she had melted completely away. Now she was willing to accept his advances because she wanted to make him happy, and herself happy as well.

"I think I'm falling in love with you, too," Momma said. "I've never been in love before, but all I know is that I want to be with you and I think of you whenever I'm not with you."

Elvis smiled his beautiful smile as he drew her closely to him. Then he kissed her head, then her check and, finally, her lips.

ONCE UPON A TIME: ELVIS AND ANITA

Chapter 4

Juggling Life with Elvis

Every afternoon that summer, Elvis called Momma and asked her over to Graceland. Once she arrived, he'd kiss her, put his arm around her and keep her at his side all evening. She was his property, so to speak — and though most of the guys in his entourage didn't know her from a hole in the ground, they were always very nice. For that matter, having all those guys constantly around Elvis (when Momma would rather have him for herself) took some getting used to. But the more they saw her, the more they got to know her, and the more comfortable Momma felt around them. In a way, hanging out at Graceland every day was like a combination of living with your family and partying with all your friends. Some days, it was absolutely great; other days, not so much.

Every so often Momma would bring along her friend Jerry Gunn and her twin sister, Kerry. Jerry and Kerry lived in Collierville, a suburb of Memphis; sometimes Momma would spend the night at their house. She and Jerry were very good friends. (Years later, Jerry Gunn was married briefly to Jerry Lee Lewis.)

Of course, when she wasn't with Elvis, Momma continued to work at the TV station. Besides hosting *Top 10 Dance Party*, she had certain responsibilities to handle each week, such as going to the local high schools and rounding up teenagers to come to the show on Saturday. Except for Saturdays (when she had to be at the station by a certain time), Momma had flexible working hours. That worked out very well, considering that she often did not come home from Graceland until the early morning hours!

Every time Momma went over to Graceland, she made sure she said hello to Elvis' parents, as well as his grandmother. Though she knew Elvis liked having her close by at all times (even if he was occupied with everyone else), she felt it was only right that she should visit with them. Before long, Elvis knew that if Momma disappeared for any length of time, he could always find her with one of his family members.

Sometimes Gladys would come in the kitchen, either to cook or just to talk with Momma, while Vernon hung out with Elvis and the guys. This is how she and Momma began to develop a close bond. Gladys absolutely adored Elvis and wanted only the best for him. She was straightforward and didn't sugarcoat anything she said. While she was happy that Elvis was a success in his career, she always worried about his safety and happiness — and always seemed happiest herself when Elvis was enjoying himself at home.

Momma also began to meet more and more of Elvis' relatives and friends. One couple she remembers well was Mr. and Mrs. Nichols. They were good friends of Gladys and Vernon and visited them frequently. Mrs. Nichols bred French poodles; in fact, that's where Elvis would get Momma's first poodle, which he would buy for her in a couple of years.

In addition, Momma met Vernon's brother, Vester, along with his wife, Cletis (who was also Gladys' sister). Uncle Vester worked at the front gate at Graceland. He and Cletis had a daughter, Patsy, who was Elvis' double first cousin. Momma and Patsy hit it off right away and they developed a very close friendship. She also met Junior and Billy Smith (both cousins of Elvis), as well as Gene Smith. Gene was the son of Gladys' sister; his wife was named Louise.

Momma liked Gene a lot and thought he was really funny — in fact, she says that when Gene and Elvis were together, they could have you in stitches for hours. The two of them had this crazy made-up language that no one else could understand, but it made you laugh like crazy! The more Momma would laugh, the more Elvis and Gene would carry on with their crazy language. Gene also could make the ugliest, weirdest old-man face that you have ever seen. Momma says that if there had ever been a talent contest for making ugly faces, Gene would have won it hands down.

One night Gene, Louise and Patsy were hanging out at Graceland with the rest of the gang when Elvis felt that everyone was in a lull. So he said, "Come on, y'all, we're going out for a while." Soon there was a caravan of cars heading downtown to Gerber's Department Store. Unbeknownst to Momma (and everyone else, for that matter), Elvis had arranged for Gerber's to be opened up after hours, just so they could shop. Sure enough, once everyone was inside the store, Elvis said, "Pick out whatever you want, it's yours."

Now, Gerber's was a very exclusive department store at the time, and as you can imagine, some people started grabbing the most expensive clothes and shoes they could find. But Momma didn't do that. She didn't want to take advantage of Elvis, or make him think that she liked him for his money. Momma wanted Elvis to know that she liked him *for him*, and nothing else.

Thinking back on it, though, she's not sure whether Elvis would have cared if she had picked out sacks and sacks of items (like many of the others did), or just the smallest trinket. He just liked to buy things for other people. He was always very generous that way.

* * *

Elvis didn't like to swim — he didn't even like the water — but that didn't stop him from enjoying his backyard pool on hot summer days. Momma remembers one particular day when, after putting on her bathing suit, she got into the water with Elvis. The two of them splashed around in the shallow end before Elvis got out and sat on a deck chair, while Momma continued swimming. After a while, Momma got out of the pool to join Elvis when he suddenly said, "Little, stop and turn around."

Momma gave him a funny look, like she didn't understand what he wanted her to do. So Elvis motioned with his fingers. "Just turn around in a circle for me." Momma did just that.

Lamar Fike was also lounging around the pool. Elvis said to him, "Lamar, now just look her over. Just look at her!" Then he asked Momma to turn around again.

"Now, do you see anything wrong with her?" Elvis continued. "Her right hip is just a little bit higher than her left hip, do you see that? Look at her little bitty feet and everything. Isn't she perfect?"

"Yeah, man, she's cool," said Lamar. "She's perfect, she's got a perfect shape. She really is *woo-hooo*!!!"

Momma thought, "Boys will be boys," but she laughed and went along with it. Then she gave them a bow and said, "Thank you, thank you, thank you, thank you." That's when Elvis got up from his chair and gave her a big kiss.

Elvis also liked to go to the fairgrounds. He'd rent it out late at night, after it was closed to the public, and invite all his friends, and anyone else who might have waiting at the gate. He and Momma rode all the rides — the Pippin, the Scrambler, the Rocket, the Bumper Cars, among others — over and over again until, as she put it, "I felt like my insides were shaking out!" But she enjoyed the fairgrounds as much as Elvis did. Sometimes he would rent it out for several nights at a time.

Though these were supposed to be private parties, somehow the press would find out, so there were always photographers around taking pictures of Elvis. Knowing that, Elvis would occasionally let a fan ride along with him, which Momma didn't mind at all. She thought that was nice, because his fans thought so much of him, and he truly appreciated them.

* * *

While Elvis was out of town, Momma went about her life as normal: going to work, shopping, visiting friends, and so forth. Being somewhat possessive, however, Elvis wanted to know where Momma was at all times, so he would call her every day and ask her to spent time with his family. Before long, it became part of Momma's routine to visit Graceland, even without Elvis there.

Of course, what Momma didn't know at the time was that Elvis was dating other women whenever he went out of town. What can I say? She was nineteen years old at the time, and still extremely naive and gullible when it came to men (and that man, in particular).

Now, this isn't to say that she did not have any suspicions later on. She did, and even confronted Elvis about it once. But we'll get to that later.

There was also the .matter of Elvis' manager, Colonel Tom Parker. He was a gruff, unpleasant man who kept people at an arm's distance, while acting like he was better than everyone else. He made it clear that he did not want Elvis to become too attached to anyone, because he thought that would ruin Elvis' career. In fact, Momma remembers that the first time she met Parker, he was at Graceland, chewing on a cigar, looking sour as always, when he let her know in no uncertain terms that he did not want her around.

But, fair is fair: Momma never cared much for Colonel Parker, either.

For that matter, Elvis was not exactly crazy about Parker himself. But he believed the Colonel knew what was best for his career, so he did what he was told. That included telling Momma what to do when it came to photographers.

"If we're photographed together, don't act like you're my girl," Elvis said. "Instead, I need you to look away or pretend you're sad. That's what Colonel Parker wants."

That hurt Momma to hear that, but she did it anyway. There are many pictures of Elvis during this time where she is in the frame, but looking off to the side. There are also many where she was actually standing near him, but stayed away from the cameras.

To his credit, Elvis seemed to understand that he was asking a lot of Momma. Once the photographers were done, he would wrap his arms around her and let her know how pleased he was that she had made the sacrifice. "You know I love you, Little," he'd say. "You are the one, and I don't care what Colonel Parker says. No matter what you read, no matter what you see, no matter what you hear, I love you, my Little, and you're the only one. Don't ever forget that."

Parker also thought it was good for Elvis to be photographed with other girls. Momma didn't like that, either — and yet it always seemed to tickle Elvis to see her in a huff. "Aw, these other girls mean nothing to me, Little," he'd say with a laugh. "It's just for publicity."

* * *

Graceland was much quieter when Elvis was away, simply because there wasn't the army of people that were always with him whenever he was around. Instead, it was just his parents, his grandmother, and Alberta the housekeeper. His cousins Travis, Billy and Bobby lived behind the house, while Uncle Vester worked at the gate. Many times Momma would go on walks with Mr. and Mrs. Presley, or sometimes sit with them by the pool.

It was during these quiet times that Momma really began to bond with Elvis' parents, and Gladys especially. They would have long conversations about living in Tupelo, and the time Vernon went to prison. Gladys said that they moved to Memphis so that Vernon could get a better job, while Vernon talked about the circumstances that sent him to prison, and how sorry he was that Gladys and Elvis had to suffer so much cruelty from others on account of him.

He regretted that his entire life, and spent every waking hour making it up to them once he was a free man.

To make her feel like she was part of the family, Mrs. Presley often showed Momma pictures of Elvis, Vernon and herself in the early days. Momma thought Gladys was still an attractive young woman, even though her health was declining. She drank a lot, plus she was much heavier than before. Most of all, she worried constantly about Elvis — that was probably the No. 1 factor behind her deteriorating health. Gladys always fretted about Elvis while he was gone, and opened up to Momma about her fears. Momma would try to comfort her and get her talking about something else.

Sometimes, when Elvis was out of town, the Presleys would take Momma for a drive, just to get out of the house. Fortunately for Gladys, Elvis was very good about calling home most every day; he'd check in with his parents first, then later on, he'd call Momma. So Gladys always had the comfort of knowing that Elvis was okay.

I mentioned before that Mrs. Presley was a straight shooter and had no problem speaking her mind. One day Momma asked if there was anybody special to Elvis before her. Sure enough, Gladys came right out and told my mother *everything*, whether she wanted to hear it or not.

First, there was Dixie Locke, who lived in the projects at Lauderdale Court. She was followed by Yvonne Lime. Mrs. Presley liked them both. Then there was Natalie Wood, who came over to the house where they used to live on Audubon. "I knew she wasn't a nice girl," Gladys said to Momma. "She would just leave her panties on the floor wherever she took them off! I didn't like that." (Momma's jaw almost dropped when she heard that. But then again, Gladys always put her cards on the table.)

After rattling off several more names, Mrs. Presley said, "And then there was Barbara Hearn." Momma knew of Miss Hearn and thought she was very, very pretty. "He liked her until he met you," Gladys said.

Of course, all this information was a bit too much for Momma, and she began to feel inadequate. After all, Elvis had seen all these girls, yet he was her very first boyfriend. But Mrs. Presley put her at ease. "Don't you worry about these other girls he's dated, Anita. All this stuff happened before. You're the one he wants."

Mrs. Presley also assured her not to worry about all the photographs of Elvis with other girls. "Elvis has to pretend he likes these other girls because the Colonel wants him to," she said. "But you're the one, never forget it."

* * *

Momma also loved spending time with Dodger, Elvis' grandmother. She was a funny, lively, down-to-earth character who could talk your ear off and spin wild tales about days gone past. She enjoyed sitting in her rocking chair with her snuff and watching soap operas. She would tell Momma to pull up a chair and watch along with her. They would talk about the characters in the show, as well as the storylines. I guess that's how Momma first became addicted to soap operas, because she still watches them today.

Momma had a great aunt that was very much like Dodger, so she connected with her instantly. She felt like she could just be herself with Dodger, as she would with her own grandmother. And, of course, she loved the wild stories she told without any reservations.

Sometimes Elvis and the guys would go out to buy firecrackers, just to fool around. Though Grandma would never presume to tell him what to do, sometimes she would say to Momma, "Elvis better watch it, or he's going to get himself in trouble."

Eventually, Momma started staying overnight at Graceland on occasion, mainly because of the late hours. She would always sleep in the bed with Dodger. Personally, I could never imagine sleeping in the same bed with my boyfriend's grandmother, no matter how much I liked her. But Momma felt completely at ease staying with Dodger, and besides they just liked each other's company.

Elvis appreciated the fact that Momma grew close to his family. He knew that sometimes people looked down upon his family because he came from such a poor background. But that thought never crossed her mind. She just thought Elvis' family were nice people, and she liked them. It was as simple as that.

* * *

Meanwhile, Momma continued to pursue her own career. She performed in the Front Street Theater production of *The Tender Trap*, at the Hotel King Cotton in Memphis. She had to kiss a guy in that play that she really didn't like, but that's why they call it acting. That being said, she was quite glad when that play completed its run.

Later that summer, she got a phone call from Frank Proctor, her former boss at WTJS. Mr. Proctor wanted Momma to enter the Hollywood Star Hunt. Though Momma really wasn't interested (she never did care for competitions), she did not want to disappoint Mr. Proctor, because he'd given her start when she hosted her radio show, *Antics of Anita*. Plus, she thought that if she did win, she might be able to spend time with Elvis in Hollywood.

On the first leg of the competition, which took place at the Strand Theater in Memphis, Momma and five other ladies (out of a total of sixty-nine entrants) were selected to represent Memphis and *The Press-Scimitar*'s circulation area in the Mid-South finals of the Hollywood Star Hunt. (Ironically, one of the other finalists was Barbara Hearn, Elvis' girlfriend just before he met Momma. That was a little awkward at first, as you might imagine, but in the end everyone was nice to each other.)

At the end of the Mid-South finals, Momma ended up tied for first place with a dancer named Portia Swaim. My mother was truly surprised by the win — she gasped, threw her arms in the air, and exclaimed thank you to all the judges. The next step was a trip to New Orleans for the finals of the Hollywood Star Hunt. Elvis wished Momma luck and said that he'd be pulling for her.

On August 27, 1957, about three days before the finals, Momma and Portia, as part of the contest winnings, went shopping at Goldsmith's to buy an outfit for New Orleans. That same night, around 11:00pm, Momma accompanied Elvis and his parents to see him off at the train station — he was heading to Washington to start a concert tour. As you can see from the photos that were taken that night, Elvis had his hand constantly on Momma; he did not want to leave her, and she didn't want him to leave, either.

They say a picture is worth a thousand words. Well, it is plain to see from these pictures that these two people were in love.

The *Memphis Press-Scimitar* reported that Elvis kissed mom a couple of times for the reporters as a small crowd of fans oohhed and ahhed, then kissed her several more times just for himself. When asked by a reporter about Momma, Elvis smiled and said, "She's No. 1 with me."

Momma could not believe her ears. After hearing him tell her so many times never to talk about their relationship in front of reporters, here he was, letting the cat out of the bag! She was truly astonished, and burst into tears as she left the station, arm in arm with his parents.

The next day, of course, the pictures were plastered all over the papers, along with the headline ELVIS' NUMBER 1 GIRL. By the time Elvis called her that night, Momma was already in New Orleans. "Well, Little, it looks like we're famous, Little. I can't pick up a paper without seeing us on the front cover." He was teasing her a little, but he was also a little upset with himself for blurting it out to the press. He also knew Colonel Parker would not be happy at all.

As you might expect, the press started giving Momma a lot of publicity. To derail the inevitable media frenzy, both she and Elvis *really* had to emphasize in interviews that they were "just friends." Again, that wasn't easy for Momma, saying and doing one thing in private, and something else in public. Probably the only other person could fully understand what she went through was Priscilla, who herself began living a double life with Elvis just a few years later.

* * *

The finals took place on August 30, 1957, at the Saenger Theater in New Orleans. Before taking the stage to sing "Walkin' After Midnight," Momma said a little prayer — not to win, but to just do her best.

My mother walked her way that night to become the winner of the Hollywood Star Hunt. When Henry Plitt of Paramount-Gulf Theaters greeted her backstage with the good news, her first words were, "Pinch me!" As part of the grand prize, she won a part in a major motion picture, as well as a seven-year movie contract.

Momma was flabbergasted — Elvis had told her many things about Hollywood, and now she was going to have a chance to experience it for herself. But what really mattered to her was that she'd be out there when he was out there. Once again, they'd be together.

Momma celebrated that night by going to the French Quarter, where she heard Sharkey and his Dixieland Band perform. When she returned to her hotel room after midnight, there was a message from Elvis. He was in Spokane, Washington, and she immediately called him back. "Hi, Honey, guess what?"

"You won, Little, you won!" Elvis said. "I told you so — I told you all along, Baby! I'm so glad... my little girl's gonna be a movie star!"

Now, truth be known, Elvis didn't really like Momma doing her own thing — what he really wanted was for her to be home and at his beck and call — but he was supportive and sweet just the same. If it were up to Momma, she would have been perfectly happy with just being at his side. But because marriage was not possible yet, she felt it was important to do something of her own.

Of course, Elvis and Momma talked about getting married many, many times, but it was always "in the future" because of his career. "I've always searched for a girl like you, Little," Elvis told her. "Most girls just fall at my feet and they will do anything, anything to get near me. They are phony as they can be. They do not care about me, all they want to do is be with me, see me, talk to me, touch me, kiss me... You're different — you're not that way at all. I really believe you do care. I don't believe you're here for the publicity. You're not here for the sex, we know that for sure. You're not here just to be seen with me."

Sometimes, they even talked about having children. Elvis wanted a boy that he could name Elvis Aaron Presley, Jr. and a girl they could name Lisa Marie Presley. Momma was happy with that name, because her name is Anita Marie.

Momma always practiced her penmanship, and it's no surprise that she still has beautiful handwriting today. One day when I was in seventh grade, we were visiting my grandmother in Jackson, Tennessee, looking through all of Momma's memorabilia that Mamaw had kept through the years. Among other things, I found this slip of paper with Momma's handwriting all over it. As young girls will often do when they are in love, she used to practice writing her name as if she were married: "Anita Marie Presley, Mrs. Elvis Aaron Presley and Mr. and Mrs. Elvis Presley." Then, much to my surprise, I also noticed that Momma had written things like: "Mr. and Mrs. Elvis Presley would like to announce the birth of their first child, Elvis Aaron Presley, Jr.," and "Mr. and Mrs. Elvis Presley would like to announce the birth of their second child, Lisa Marie Presley."

Of course, we all know what happened years later, once Elvis did have a daughter. Did it bother Momma that he ended up naming her Lisa Marie? This might surprise you to hear this, but no, not in the least. She knew that he really liked that name, and so that was that.

I, on the other hand, thought it was huge — so huge, in fact, that it freaked me out! "Momma, you have never told me this before," I said. "I can't believe that you and Elvis were going to name your child Lisa Marie! I can't believe that he *still* named her that!"

Then again, Momma didn't, and still doesn't, understand the extent of interest people have about her life with Elvis. It astonishes her that, even after all these years, people still ask her for interviews. The way she sees it, her life is no different than yours or mine. Even though Elvis was her first love, they were just two people in love in their youth, and now he's gone. Remembering these years certainly brings her back to many happy moments together... but it also awakens memories of sad times that she would just as soon forget..

Arm in arm before Elvis departs on the train.
(Courtesy of www.bobkleinmedia.com)

Gazing deeply into each other's eyes as if no one else were around them.
(Courtesy of Memphis Press-Scimitar)

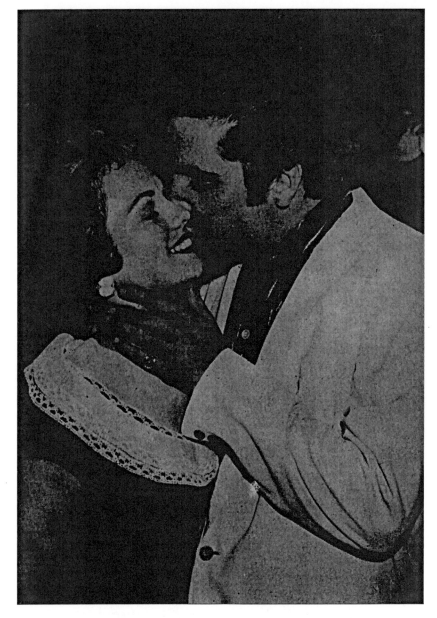

Elvis was at the train station in Memphis leaving for a tour of the northwest when he called Anita his "No. 1 Girl." *(Courtesy of Brian Petersen)*

Love is in the air!
(Courtesy of Brian Petersen)

Walking hand in hand to the train station for their fond farewell!
(Courtesy of Cristian Otopeanu)

Gladys looking on with approval at the goodbye that never seemed to end.
(Courtesy of Claude Francisci)

Anita leaving Graceland, looking away from the camera
as she was often instructed to do. *(From the collection of Anita Wood)*

Though normally low key, even Anita (in white gown) could not resist showing her glee at
winning the Mid-South Hollywood Star Hunt when she threw her arms in the air and
squealed "Thank you!" *(Photo by William Leaptrott, Memphis Press-Scimitar)*

Chapter 5

First Trip to Hollywood

Momma flew to Hollywood on Saturday, September 7, 1957. Though she was nervous as always about being on a plane, there were plenty of other things going on to keep her distracted. For one, many of the passengers on the plane recognized her from TV, as well as from her picture in the paper. Among these fans were a group of Brazilian Air Force men, who were en route to Lackland Air Force Base. They asked for Momma's autograph. She happily obliged, then smiled and answered questions about her, and about Elvis.

Momma was also excited, of course, about the trip itself. She was on her way to being a movie star, and her mother, especially, was elated. But the biggest lift Momma got was from knowing that, in just a few short hours, she would be with her honey again. It had been ten days since she last saw him (which can be an eternity when you're nineteen years old), and yet so much had happened. By now Elvis was in Hollywood, having just completed his Northwest Coast tour. They were about to spend a few precious days together before he had to hit the road again, and she could not wait to see him.

Some fans wanted to know if Elvis would be greeting Momma at the airport when she landed in Hollywood. "Oh, no," she said, without getting into any specifics. The reason why, as you may have guessed, is that Elvis knew that he'd be mobbed if he were there, and he didn't want any publicity. Instead, he told Momma to call him at the Beverly Wilshire Hotel once she got settled, and then he'd pick her up. That turned out to be shrewd thinking, because as soon as Momma stepped off the plane, there were photographers all over the place.

Bickford Webber, an assistant to Paramount-Gulf Theaters AB-PT Pictures president Irving Levin, met Momma at the airport and whisked her away to the Knickerbocker Hotel. She settled into her room, freshened up a bit, and then gave Elvis a call. A few minutes later, Elvis pulled up in a rented station wagon, along with Lamar Fike and George Klein, to pick her up for a night of sight-seeing. They drove around almost all night. Elvis showed her Grauman's Chinese Theater, Ciro's, Mocambo, all the beautiful homes in Beverly Hills, and many other famous places, including some of the oil wells that were once part of the L.A. landscape.

Late Sunday morning Elvis sent a car to pick Momma up and bring her back to the Beverly Wilshire Hotel, where they ate breakfast on the terrace of his penthouse. Momma had never been in a penthouse, and was quite amazed at how large and elaborate it was. In fact, it seemed almost regal to her. Beyond that, however, she can't remember too many details about the room, because her eyes were fixed on Elvis.

After breakfast, Elvis had all sorts of activities planned for the day, including a trip to the RCA-Victor studios, where he had just recorded "Don't" only two days before. Momma thought it was just wonderful (and if you've never heard this song before, I think you'll agree). She also listened to his soon-to-be-released Christmas album, which she also thought was marvelous and unlike anything she'd ever heard before.

Elvis then gave Momma a tour of MGM studios, where he had recently filmed *Jailhouse Rock*, with a promise to bring her back the next day for a special screening of the picture, well before it was released to the public. Momma quickly discovered that Elvis liked going to the movies in Hollywood just as much as he did in Memphis, because they saw four together that afternoon: *The Giant Claw, The Day the World Exploded, Calypso Heat Wave,* and *3:10 to Yuma.* Of the four, Momma liked *3:10 to Yuma* the best (even though it was a Western).

All in all, it was a great day, except for the strange stop they made at a pharmacy before returning to Elvis' hotel room. That's when Momma found out about the safe that Elvis kept in the trunk of the car. It was square, not exactly large (but not exactly small, either), and very heavy — so heavy, in fact, that it took two of the guys to move it.

Elvis had this medical book about different drugs, and what they did. Momma could tell that he had gone through this book cover to cover, because he had marked up different pages that talked about certain drugs that he thought might help him in some way: diet pills, vitamins, sleeping pills, wake up pills, sinus pills, and just about any other pill you can think of. There were even pills that were supposed to help you get a tan easier, of all things! (Momma does not believe any narcotics were involved, but she cannot recall for sure.) So while the guys brought the safe up to the counter, Elvis talked to the pharmacist about the various drugs that he'd read about in the book. The pharmacist said, in effect, "Help yourself." By the time Elvis was finished picking out what he wanted, the safe was completely full.

Later that Sunday night, when Momma returned to her hotel room, she decided to write a letter to her mother and family. This was the first time she'd been this far from home by herself, and there were so many things she wanted to tell them:

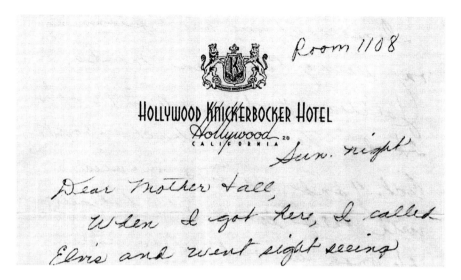

Room 1108

HOLLYWOOD KNICKERBOCKER HOTEL
Hollywood
C A L I F O R N I A   29
Sun. night

Dear Mother & all,
When I got here, I called Elvis and went sight seeing

Dear Mother & all,

When I got here, I called Elvis and went sight seeing with him Sat. night. I spent the day Sun. with him, even had breakfast with him. I don't start work until tomorrow. We saw 4 movies today and went to MGM lot & RCA Victor studios & listened to Elvis' records. But Elvis is leaving Mon. night (tomorrow) because his Uncle Travis is very ill and in the hospital and then too, Duke died this morning.

Tomorrow, we are planning on seeing Elvis' new movie, Jailhouse Rock, in MGM lot He has to come back about Oct. 7 and do two movies, with only two weeks between. He may be out here during Xmas. Maybe I can come back in Oct. or Nov. I sure wish you were here. I have twin beds & we could make it fine, as I haven't spent one cent yet. I don't like being alone at all!! It sure is hot here! Not very cool.

I'll write again soon.

Love to Daddy, Jerry, Joe and Andy,
Mamaw, Papaw, & Grandmother,
Lonesome Anita

"Duke," in case you're wondering, was Elvis' dog at that time. Elvis enjoyed animals, and he had several pets throughout their relationship.

* * *

The next day, Monday, Momma met with some representatives from AB-PT Pictures about *Girl in the Woods*, the film in which she was to appear as a result of winning the Hollywood Star Hunt contest. Elvis gave her a lot of pointers about what to say and do, which she appreciated. When the meeting let out, Momma, knowing that Elvis was leaving that night and that this would be their last day together in Hollywood, asked for the rest of the day off. The studio granted her request.

When Momma returned to Elvis' suite, she gave him a rundown of the meetings, the gist of which was she would have a one-line speaking part, and get to sing one song. Elvis felt like they were taking advantage of her; he thought they weren't paying her enough money and that her part was much too small. "They promised you more than that in the contest," he said. "You have to stand up for yourself, Little. Don't let them run all over you, because they will try to do that."

Again, Momma appreciated everything he said. But at the moment, all she cared about was that she and Elvis were about to spend the rest of the day together.

As he had promised, Elvis took Momma back to MGM Studios to see *Jailhouse Rock*, which she enjoyed, especially the dance scenes and the music. Of all the songs Elvis sang in that picture, his favorite was "Young and Beautiful," but he also liked "Don't Leave Me Now" and "Treat Me Nice." Ironically, with all the shaking and moving that Elvis did on stage, he never felt like he knew how to dance, so he was particularly proud about his dance work in this movie. He thought it was pretty sharp that he learned to dance with a group, plus he liked the sequence where he slid down a fireman's pole.

Elvis liked making *Jailhouse Rock* because he thought it gave him more of an opportunity to act. He also enjoyed working with Mickey Shaughnessy, whom he thought was a really good actor. But watching the movie also made him sad. Just two months earlier, around the time he started seeing Momma, Elvis learned that Judy Tyler, his leading lady in *Jailhouse Rock*, had died in a terrible car accident with her husband. Elvis was terribly upset by the news, and he commented about Judy while he and Momma were watching the movie.

* * *

Later that night, as Elvis was packing his things for the trip home, Momma and the guys were chatting in the living room of his penthouse suite when he asked her to come to the bedroom. He had a little box in his hand, and a big grin on his face, yet he also seemed a little nervous. "This is for you," he said.

Inside the box was a huge gold ring, with a diamond in the center surrounded by eighteen sapphires, plus lots of gold in an overlaying leaf type design under the circle of gems. An intricate gold-braided rope ran along the center of the leaves. It was the largest, most beautiful ring my mother had ever seen. No one had ever given her anything so extravagant.

Elvis presented the ring to Momma and kissed her. Then he took her right hand in his and said, "Let's put it on your right finger and call it a friendship ring. I know Colonel Parker doesn't want people to get the wrong idea and think that we're more than friends — but this is really our ring, Little. This means that we're really close and just remember that I gave it to you."

Then he hugged her and kissed her again and said, "I hope you like it."

This was the first of several rings that Elvis would give Momma over the years — but the smile on his face that night is a memory she will never forget.

That may be why, even though she gave away almost everything else Elvis had given her once she married my daddy, she kept this ring in her family. Momma gave it to her mother, who wore the ring for many years until after I was married, when it was then given to me. I wear it most days on the third finger of my right hand, just like Momma had worn it so many years ago. It's a nice memento, and people love to look at it when they first find out my mom's story.

Momma and Elvis were so excited about the ring, they went out to the living room area so that they could show it off to the guys. "Look at what I bought for Little," Elvis said.

Judging from their reactions, this had to be the first time Elvis had ever given anyone such an expensive gift — and a ring at that! All they could say was "Wow!" and "Where'd you get that ring?!" and "Ohh, that is so pretty!" Every now and then, the guys would also give each other "the eyes," like there was really something going on that wasn't being said.

Elvis, in the meantime, was beside himself with joy. He kept taking Momma by the hand and saying things like, "That sure is a pretty ring on your finger. I wonder where you got that?"

But then, suddenly, the happy moment took an awkward turn. Momma was showing off the ring to the others when Tommy, one of the guys in Elvis' group that came with him to Hollywood, approached her from behind, put his arms around her and said something like, "Oh, that's such a beautiful ring, Anita, I know you're so excited."

It was all very innocent — and yet, when Elvis noticed them from across the room, he lost control. He immediately grabbed Tommy by the shoulder, and told him to get his hands off her. Elvis then ordered Momma to *"Get over there,"* pointing to the side of the room. When she didn't respond quickly enough to his liking, he actually picked her up and moved her himself. Then he continued to chew out Tommy: "Don't you ever touch her again!"

Tommy tried to explain that he was just looking at the ring, but Elvis would have none of that. "You pack your clothes now," he said. "I want you on the next plane to Memphis."

Momma knew that Elvis was possessive, but this was the first time she'd ever seen his bad side — and she was surprised by how fierce and explosive his temper could be. Most of all, she was embarrassed, because there was really nothing to it. But that's how protective and jealous Elvis could be, and nothing she could have said or done in that moment would have changed his mind.

The other thing Momma learned about Elvis' temper is that once he exploded, it was over. Sure enough, he walked over to where she was, gave her a kiss, and started talking as if nothing had happened. Everyone else in the room followed suit.

A short while later, Elvis took Momma back to her hotel, where they said their goodbyes. It was difficult for both of them because they didn't want to be separated, and Elvis really didn't want her to stay in Hollywood alone. "Little, I really want you to come with me," he said. He knew that Hollywood was as far removed from Memphis as could be, and he was nervous about leaving her there. But he also knew that this was a good opportunity for her, and encouraged her to pursuit it. He did, however, tell her to be careful, to stay in her room until the studio sent a car for her, and to not go out to do *anything* by herself.

Then he kissed her and promised that he would call her just as soon as he got to Memphis... which he did.

* * *

Momma spent the next day in meetings with studio representatives in publicity, wardrobe, and production. It was a long, long day, and being by herself in this strange town without any family or friends, she was feeling lonely and miserable by the time Elvis called. He must have been worrying a lot about her himself, because by the time he called her again on Thursday, he had decided that he wanted her to come home, regardless of the opportunity that awaited her in Hollywood. In fact, he had already made the arrangements for her to fly back to Memphis the very next day, Friday, September 13.

As it happened, *Girl in the Woods* was not scheduled to begin production until Monday, September 23. So when Momma asked Mr. Levin for permission to go home to Memphis (well, really to Elvis), he said yes. (However, Mr. Levin did tell Momma that he wanted her to "lose her Southern accent" by the time she came back. How do you lose an accent you've had for nineteen years in two weeks, for goodness sake?!)

On Friday, September 13, Elvis picked Momma up at the Memphis airport himself — which, as I say, was something he never did. And yet, he was so happy that she had chosen to leave Hollywood behind and come home to him, that there he was, waiting for her at the gate as her flight came in. As you may have guessed, when Momma stepped off the plane and saw Elvis standing at the bottom of the steps, she could hardly believe her eyes! She ran down the stairs with glee and threw herself into his outstretched arms.

Of course, photographers were there to capture the moment. But as you can see from the pictures, there is no denying that Momma and Elvis were madly in love.

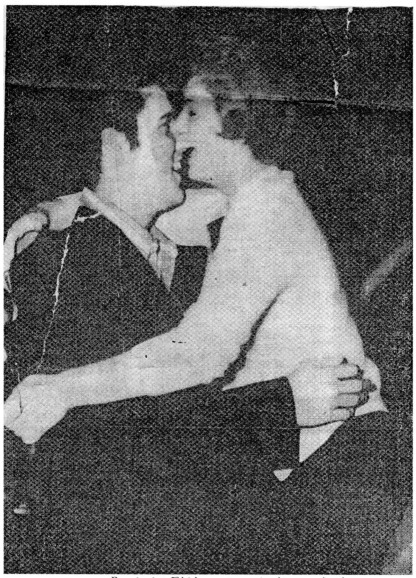

Running into Elvis' arms, too overjoyed to remember the photographers were there, just a few moments.

DAR-R-R-LING! – REUNION AT THE AIRPORT
was the headline in the *Memphis Press-Scimitar*.
(Photo by William Leaptrott/Memphis Press-Scimitar)

THAT LONG, LONG LOOK and entwined fingers.
(Courtesy of Memphis Press-Scimitar)

Chapter 6

Home Base

Back in Memphis, Momma learned that two of Elvis' band members, Bill and Scotty, had quit. He was very upset about that, and she did her best to console him. That wasn't always easy, because Elvis didn't like to talk about any bad stuff with Momma. But at the same time, he knew that he could be as carefree with her as she grew to be with him. So when he did open up, she gave him a chance to let go of his worries, at least for a while.

Besides, there were times when Elvis had to reassure her, too. It wasn't easy having to share your boyfriend with so many other people. Part of this had to do with the fact that Elvis simply did not like to be alone, *ever*. Whether this came from some deep-seeded fear, I don't know, but Momma said that Elvis always, *always* had people around.

Still, there were moments — particularly whenever Elvis invited fans at the gate to come up to the house (or anywhere, really), and female fans would try to get close to him and touch him — then Momma would feel jealous or possessive or frustrated, just as anyone else would have felt, if they were her. Elvis seemed very mindful of that, and always did his best to give her the reassurance that a girl would need. He was very persuasive, and always convinced Momma of his true love for her, and her alone, usually with the help of some baby talk: "Are you jealous, Little? You are so adorable when you're jealous. You know 'him yuvs her and her yuvs him.'" Then he'd cuddle her and kiss her check, ear, and head, until she was no longer mad at him. Then he'd kiss her on the lips.

* * *

With all the running around Momma had to do, Elvis worried about how reliable her old car was. So one night, after picking her up and bringing her to Graceland, he told her that he wanted her to drive one of his cars home. It was a big white Imperial hardtop convertible.

"Oh, Elvis, I couldn't possibly ask you to do that," Momma said.

"I insist, Little," he said. "I just want you to be safe. Besides, I have no use for it anyway."

So Momma started driving Elvis' convertible all around Memphis, as well as to her parents' house in Jackson, Tennessee. As you might imagine, with a car like that, everywhere she went, it caused quite a stir. There were always people gathering around to ask her questions, or simply to take pictures.

Momma felt that Mrs. Patty was concerned about the late hours she was keeping, so she moved into an apartment with some girlfriends. Truth be told, however, she mostly used it as a place to keep some of her clothes. The more time she spent with Elvis and his family, the more they continued to insist that she spend the night with them at Graceland. For all intents and purposes, it became as much a "home base" for my mother as it was for Elvis.

Elvis and Momma continued to talk about getting married some day, and having children together at Graceland. Though it was always centered on "some day," because they were both still very young and Elvis was at the peak of his career, Momma was completely OK with that, and was prepared to wait until the time was right. (They did, however, share their plans with Elvis' parents, who were both delighted at the idea.)

As far as Momma knew, Elvis was all she could ask for in a future husband: he was funny, good-looking, affectionate, loving and romantic, and he wasn't on too much medication. Yes, he had a temper, and he could explode over little things. But she never saw him do anything as erratic as shoot a television, as rumor would have it.

Momma also liked that Elvis was a Christian, just as she was. Every now and then they'd have spiritual conversations about their beliefs in God. She told Elvis about when she was saved and how that changed her life. He told Momma that he and his family used to go to church all the time when he was a little boy in Tupelo, and that he even sang in the choir. Going to church every Sunday was something he missed being able to do.

Elvis tried to be what he considered to be "good," though he often talked to Momma about not always being as "good" as he should. He also had certain ideas of what was bad and what wasn't. For instance, Elvis thought drinking alcohol was a bad thing, so he didn't drink (at least, not while Momma was around him). As far as their physical relationship was concerned, he thought as long as they did not have actual intercourse, then everything was okay.

Of course, the more time Momma spent with Elvis, the stronger her feelings for him grew, and the more intense their physical relationship became.

Momma remembers the first night she slept in that huge bed of his. She was getting ready to go to bed in Grandma's room when Elvis said, "Little, I would like you to please come up and sleep with me tonight because I don't want to be alone."

Of course, he knew how Momma felt about that, and he assured her that nothing would happen. "I promise I will not touch you. I just need you to be up there in the room with me."

My mom knew that Elvis had some of the guys sleep on the floor in his room from time to time. She also knew that he always took a sleeping pill before he went to bed that knocked him out. So she went up to Dodger's room, gathered some clothes, and then walked to Elvis' bedroom. There, she changed into baby doll pajamas in his bathroom, then slowly, and very shyly, came back into his room.

By this time, Elvis was already in the bed covered up, wearing only his underwear. He was reading a book, but put it down to watch her come to him. She climbed into that huge bed on the opposite side of Elvis, and laid down.

"Why, Little, you're too far away," Elvis said with a smile. "Come over here. I want to at least touch you with my foot." That made her laugh, and she moved a little closer to him.

Like he promised, Elvis did not try to get sexual in any way — he only put his arm around Momma, and soon fell sound asleep.

Momma has always had trouble sleeping, and that night was no exception. She laid there for what seemed like forever, looking around the room, wondering who's been there before her, and who's going to be there next. Eventually, though, she realized that it didn't really matter, because she was the one who was there *right now*, next to the love of her life. With that, she happily closed her eyes and went to sleep.

After this night, Momma began sleeping in Elvis' bed when he was home, and with Dodger when he wasn't. Over time, Elvis started cuddling her more before he fell asleep, and very slowly became more intimate — but only to a point, and always stopping before intercourse.

* * *

It was during this time that Momma grew particularly close to Mr. and Mrs. Presley, Patsy (Elvis' double first cousin), Louise (wife of Elvis' cousin Gene) and, of course, Dodger, Elvis' grandma. In fact, Momma spent so much time with Dodger that they became great friends. Dodger was just down to earth and naturally funny. She loved to sit and talk, especially about Elvis and the future, and what Elvis was like as a little boy. She was also as much a night owl as Elvis, and she liked to watch television with Momma into the wee hours of the morning. Grandma had a king size bed (maybe even a Hollywood king), and she would sleep on one side, with Momma on the other.

Momma also spent a lot of time talking to Gladys downstairs in the kitchen, often while she was cooking greens and other country foods that my mother grew to love. Gladys would say all the time, "Nita, I can just see you and Elvis married now and that little ole boy, that little ole blond-headed Elvis boy, running up and down that driveway patting his little feet on the asphalt — and we would name him Junior, Elvis Presley Jr." (Of course, as I mentioned before, they also talked about having a girl, whom they would name Lisa Marie.) Gladys' face would always light up whenever she thought the possibility of grandchildren. She was so open and honest with her feelings. It was incredibly endearing and sweet.

Gladys even talked about this once with my own grandmother, when she came by Graceland to pick up Momma for a singing engagement in Arkansas. "I wish Elvis and Anita would go ahead and get married," Gladys told Mamaw. "I want to have a little grandbaby!"

"Well, who knows?" Mamaw said. "Maybe they will."

Sometimes Gladys also talked to Momma about Jesse Garon, Elvis' twin brother, who had died at birth. That was a difficult subject, as it would be for any mother who had lost a child, and yet she seemed comfortable discussing it with Momma. For one, it explained why she was so very close to Elvis, and why she always fretted about him getting hurt. He may have been The King in the eyes of the rest of the world, but to her, he was still her baby. In fact, sometimes when talking about Elvis, Gladys would slip into "baby talk," especially when telling Momma stories about when he was a little boy.

Now Vernon, on the other hand, was a little more reserved with his emotions. He was always thinking about money and what Elvis should do next for his career. But that doesn't mean he was not affectionate in his own way. He always called Momma "Neeter" (which is the same nickname that my daddy's parents would give her a few years later), and he had his moments where he would let loose.

One time, when Momma had a chest cold, Vernon came into Dodger's room, where Momma was in bed, and gave her a jar of ointment. "Look, Neeter, you see this stuff right here? You just rub some of it on your chest and you will feel so much better."

Momma thanked him and did what he said, only to find that the stuff made her chest burn like crazy. She immediately started walking around the room, fanning herself while squealing, "This is awful hot!"

For some reason, Vernon thought that was awfully funny, and before Momma knew it, he was laughing as hard as Elvis would if he were in the room. Dodger was laughing, too, only she was a little more reassuring. "Don't worry, Anita. Just give it a minute and it'll stop burning."

Then again, Elvis liked to pull pranks, too. One of his favorites was hiding behind a door or sneaking up behind Momma to scare her. Every time he did that, she'd holler at him, and say, "Don't do that! You're going to give me a heart attack!"

Elvis also liked to trick Momma into saying words that usually were vulgar in nature. Having grown up extremely sheltered, Momma had never heard most curse words before, so she had no idea what she was really saying (which, of course, made Elvis and the guys fall out of their seats laughing). She was always embarrassed later on, once she found out what the words meant!

* * *

In the meantime, Momma was still in high demand in the Memphis area. One of her regular gigs was modeling dinner shows for Goldsmith's Department Store. These shows were great, because all she had to do was walk around modeling clothes that she would later have the option to buy at a much reduced price.

Knowing that Elvis was not always keen about her doing her own thing, I asked my mom what he thought of her doing these shows. To my surprise, she told me that he actually liked it, because they had nothing to do with him — it was just something Anita Wood was doing. Anything that did not directly link her to Elvis was a good thing, because it helped steer the media away from him. Knowing that, whenever Momma was asked to model or sing, she would gladly accept the offer. After all, it helped her make a living for herself.

Momma was also asked to officiate the launching of the sternwheeler for the Mid-South Fair, which was held in Memphis on September 20-28, 1957. For this event, Momma was asked to pose standing on a boat for a publicity photograph. The photo shoot went off without a hitch — but when it was time to get off the boat, things took a dive for the worse. The president of the fair, Wallace Witmer, gallantly lifted Momma up, carried her carefully over a makeshift gang plank, and put her safely on the shore. Unfortunately for Mr. Witmer, at that moment, the plank gave way, and he fell right into the lagoon! Elvis got a real kick out of that when Momma told him what had happened.

Momma loved doing the fair — that's where she got the biggest break in her career. On Wednesday, September 25, 1957, she performed twice at the fair's "Teen Town" section, where she danced the Bop with teenagers and signed autographs on everything from shoes, hats, teddy bears, even body parts! She also sang at a fair fashion show, as well as performed at the finals of the Fair's Youth Talent Show on Saturday, September 28, after filming *Top 10 Dance Party*. She also managed to squeeze in appearances at the Tennessee Association of Real Estate Board's luncheon, as well as Cathy Bauby's television show.

Elvis went to the fair with Momma twice that week — once when it was raining, and hardly anybody was there; and another time very late, after most people had already left. Because of Elvis' soaring notoriety, this was one of the last times they could go anywhere like that together, like any other couple would. As mentioned before, once Elvis was spotted, his fans couldn't help but start talking to him — and because Elvis couldn't bring himself to be rude and cut them off, that could go forever. But on these occasions, the fans couldn't have been sweeter. One fan, in fact, who recognized Momma gave her a huge teddy bear that he had just won.

Momma also accompanied Elvis to Tupelo for his "homecoming performance" at the Mississippi-Alabama Fair. This was the first time she would see him perform live and, of course, she thought he was very talented, magnetic, almost like magic, with a great stage presence that left the crowd absolutely mesmerized. Meanwhile, Elvis kept flirting with her from the stage, looking at her every so often as he sang.

Backstage before the show, a reporter asked Elvis if he had found anyone special. He looked at Momma apologetically for a second, then answered, "No, not yet." Once the press had left, however, Elvis reminded her that he had to say that, simply for publicity purposes: "Don't get upset, Little. You know I love you and that you're the only one for me."

While Momma appreciated hearing that, it did not completely take away the sting of those words. In fact, once she was back in Memphis, a group of fans asked her if what Elvis had said in the papers was really true. "Yes," she replied, "but we're the same friends we've always been. I sometimes wish I hadn't gone with him to Tupelo."

Of course, there were a few things going on when Elvis was out of town that Momma didn't know about — if there weren't, she never would have wished that she hadn't accompanied him to Tupelo. But again, we'll get to that later.

* * *

Meanwhile, Momma was still under contract to William Platt with AB-PT Theaters, so she also had to perform at events throughout the country that he would set up for her. In those days actors and singers would often perform live at movie theaters whenever a new picture opened — this, in addition to singing in nightclubs, making television appearances, showing up for the opening of a new supermarket, or any other event the publicity department might think of. In that respect, Mr. Platt was basically Momma's manager, and he certainly kept her busy.

During this time Elvis again told Momma that he had second thoughts about her pursuing a movie career. He didn't mind if she sang (and, in fact, he often helped her pick out songs), but he didn't want her to do any love scenes — which, considering how young and beautiful she was, he knew would surely come her way if she continued to do movies. "Making movies could turn into a serious situation, Little," he said. "I know there have been many times where stars have fallen for their co-stars. You have to watch that."

He should have taken his own advice, if you ask me.

Fortunately for Elvis, Momma was perfectly content with just being his girl, so it wasn't a hard decision for her. To keep Elvis happy, she informed Mr. Platt that she didn't want to do *Girl in the Woods* (or any other movie, for that matter). Personally, I don't think that was the best decision she could have made. But, as they say, things happen for a reason.

In the meantime, while Elvis went on tour in Hollywood, Las Vegas, and Hawaii, Momma performed at the 18th Annual National Cotton Picking Contest in Blytheville, Arkansas; at the world premiere of *Eighteen and Anxious* in New Orleans; at a two-day Cerebral Palsy Fund telethon in Youngstown, Ohio; and at a ceremony in Austin, Texas, where she was named an Honorary Texas Citizen.

With each trip, she would fly into the location, make her appearance, then immediately fly back to Memphis.

On one of these trips a certain actor who shall remain nameless came by my mother's hotel room one night. Like her, he was a contract player for AB-PT, and was in town for some promotional appearance. Momma had just finished dressing for bed when she heard a knock on her door. At first, she was startled; she hadn't ordered anything from room service, and she certainly wasn't expecting anyone. But when she looked through the peephole, she felt relieved, because she and the actor knew each other. She put on her robe, opened the door, and wondered what he needed.

He walked right past her, headed straight for her bed, and started taking his clothes off. He smelled like he had been drinking.

Momma was confused at first, but once she realized what he was up to, she immediately put a stop to it: *"You get out of my room, right this minute!"*

He looked at her as if she was crazy, but beyond muttering something derogatory under his breath, nothing happened. He gathered his clothes and left.

Momma didn't dare mention this to Elvis — knowing that white hot temper of his, she was afraid he might've killed the man. She will not even tell me who this actor is because he still works in the industry today, and she does not want to hurt him or his family in any way.

Elvis could be very jealous around Momma, even when he had no reason to. One time, he, Momma and the boys went out to the airport to watch the airplanes land and lift off. Along with them was Elvis' friend Nick Adams (the actor, but *not* the one mentioned in the story above). Since Nick was visiting from out of town, Momma was being friendly to him, like a good hostess would; beyond that, she had no interest in him whatsoever. Nevertheless, Elvis didn't like the sight of that, so he grabbed her by the shoulders, shook her, and said, "You stay away from him and stop talking!"

Of course, Momma was shocked; she didn't think that she had done anything wrong. But that's how insecure Elvis could be. He demanded loyalty and devotion to him above all else — and if he felt slighted in any way, he would immediately let you know it.

* * *

Given her obligations with AB-PT, it soon became evident that Momma could no longer keep staying up all night with Elvis and the boys, while working all day and making appearances out of town. Something had to give, and eventually she gave up her co-hosting duties on *Top 10 Dance Party*. (Wink Martindale, by the way, continued hosting *Dance Party* until March 1959, when he left for Hollywood. George Klein then stepped in as host of the show, which became known as *Talent Party*.)

71

Still, Momma felt it was important that she have some sort of job — not only to earn money on her own, but to keep herself from being bored whenever Elvis was away on tour. So Elvis asked his friend who ran the Malco Theater to hire her as a part-time assistant. It was office work, mostly (filing, typing, and doing odd jobs), which Momma knew diddly squat about, but she's a quick study and she learned. The best part about it, as far as Elvis was concerned, was that she only had to go to work when he was out of town. (Elvis wanted Momma available at all times when he was in Memphis without the restrictions of a steady job.)

In the meantime, Elvis was always on the lookout for new things to do together. At some point he started renting out the Rainbow Roller Skating Rink all night, after closing hours. The guys would come along, of course (and, on occasion, so would Patsy). Of course, if there were still kids at the rink when they got there, Elvis would invite them to stay and skate with him, along with however many fans were waiting at the gate when everyone left Graceland. Elvis would buy knee pads and elbow pads for everyone to wear.

Momma was a good skater, but she was always a lady first. Elvis liked to make these long "cat tails," with him at the head, and everyone else holding on to the person in front of them. They'd whip the line so fast, it seemed like 90 miles per hour — and sometimes the last few people at the end would get slung off and land hard on their backsides! (Fortunately, no one ever got badly hurt.) Momma, however, had no interest in doing anything rough like that.

Nor did she share Elvis' interest in pills. One night, before heading out to the rink, she and Patsy were feeling especially tired. Elvis took a green-and-white capsule, cut it in half, and told them each to take half. While it did keep her up the rest of the night, Momma never did anything like that again. She just didn't like the way it made her feel.

One night, there were some teenage girls waiting at the gate. Elvis invited them inside, and before long they were all wrestling and tickling each other, as if they were young children. (The girls were never one on one with Elvis, but always in a group together.) Naturally, Momma didn't care for that, but she didn't let it bother her too much. She looked at the girls as if they were kids, and not as a threat at all.

Now, when he invited these girls upstairs to his bedroom... that was a different story. "Oh, Little, we're just going to play," he said. "Nothing's going to happen."

To this day, my mother cannot believe how much control Elvis had over her. But, then again, he had such a magnetic personality, he had that effect on everyone. He could tell you something was red when it was actually white, and somehow you'd believe it.

She must have learned her lesson, though, because she raised me never to take any such nonsense from any boyfriend. She also taught me never to chase after a boy, or wait around for one, either — if he wanted another girl, then he could have her!

* * *

Still, life with Elvis rolled along until that dreadful day in December 1957, when he received his draft notice from the U.S. Army. It was the last thing in the world anyone had expected.

Momma was with him when he got the news, and she remembers how it tore him up inside. Not that he didn't want to serve his country — he did (Elvis was *very* patriotic). Even though different branches of the military offered him special services, he declined, saying he wanted to be a regular soldier. But a two-year stint as a regular soldier would also mean that he'd have to put his career on hold. All the momentum that he had worked so hard to build, was about to come to a screeching halt.

That's hard to accept for *any* performer, let alone the King of Rock 'n' Roll. Momma can still see him holding that letter, shaking his head as he read it over and over again.

Elvis was also afraid of what this would do to his mother. He asked Momma to come with him as he broke the news to her.

Gladys was beside herself. "Oh my Lord, son, what are we going to do?" she cried. "I can't believe you have to go in the Army! No... *no, this is not right*. I don't want you to go! I'm so frightened! We will try to get you out."

Elvis hugged his mother. "Things will be okay, Momma," he said as he wiped away her tears. "This is something I need to do."

Vernon also put his arm around Gladys. "It'll be all right," he said. "We'll do what we have to do."

Elvis also promised his mother that she would go with him wherever he was stationed, which she did when he went to Texas — and would have followed him to Germany as well, had she lived. (Oh, how things might have turned out differently, if she had lived.)

Still, it was a very, very emotional scene that night, with a lot of tears and hugging. At one point the entire family huddled together with their arms around each other: Elvis holding Gladys and Momma on one side, while Vernon embraced them from the other. Despite the panic that hung over the room, everyone tried to assure each other, and Gladys especially, that everything would be all right.

It was a pivotal moment in that family's life, and my mother was there to share it with them. If she had any lingering doubts about how the Presleys felt about her, this wiped them all away.

Eventually, Gladys pulled herself together, and everyone else calmed down. At that point, Elvis decided to take Momma for a ride so that he could clear his head a bit.

Nevertheless, my mom believes this is when Gladys' health began taking a turn for the worse. She was always fearful about Elvis' future. Now that he was about to step into a great big unknown, she worried even more than ever before, if that was even possible.

Anita's plane trip to Hollywood.
(Courtesy of Memphis Press-Scimitar Morgue Files/
Special Collections, University of Memphis Libraries)

Glad to see each other when Elvis surprised Anita
by showing up at the airport when she returned from Hollywood.
(Courtesy of Memphis Press-Scimitar)

Anita's "friendship ring" from Elvis.
(Courtesy of Memphis Press-Scimitar Morgue Files/
Special Collections, University of Memphis Libraries)

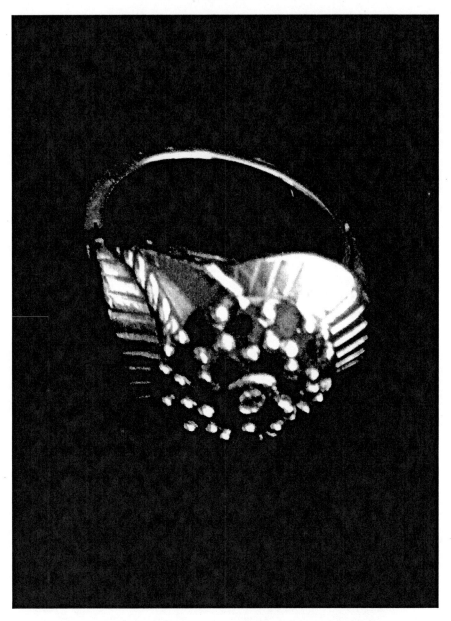

Close-up of Anita's "friendship ring," which Jonnita wears today

Mr. Wallace Witmer, Mid-South Fair president, and Mrs. Patty
were at the airport to meet Anita and present her with a gold pass to the fair.
No one expected Elvis to be there. *(Courtesy of Brian Petersen)*

Anita, Elvis and the guys leaving the airport after their sweet reunion.
(Courtesy of Russ Howe)

Another snapshot of Anita and Elvis at the Memphis airport. *(Courtesy of Julian Keen)*

Leaving airport, laughing, hand in hand. (*Courtesy of Brian Petersen*)

Elvis "baby-talking" Anita after she returns home
from Hollywood. (*Courtesy of Brian Petersen*)

After their reunion at the Memphis Airport, Elvis kept picking up
Anita's hand and marveling at her ring. (*Courtesy of Brian Petersen*)

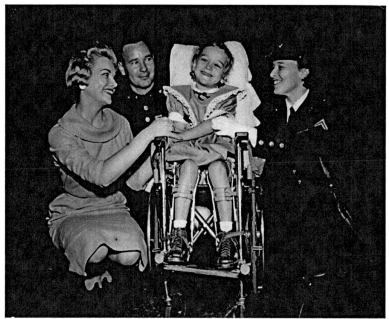

Anita in Youngstown, Ohio for a two-day Cerebral Palsy Fund telethon.
(From the collection of Anita Wood)

Mr. Witmer taking a splash after posing with Anita for the Fair's Sternwheeler. *(Courtesy of Memphis Press-Scimitar)*

Anita dancing the Bop with fans
at the Mid-South Fair's Teen Town
(Courtesy of Memphis Press-Scimitar Morgue Files/
Special Collections, University of Memphis Libraries)

Anita looking down as Elvis looks back at her while telling the reporters that there wasn't anyone special in his life. *(Courtesy of Memphis Press-Scimitar)*

Elvis "baby talking" Anita after downplaying their relationship to the press at Tupelo. *(Courtesy of www.bobkleinmedia.com)*

Honorary Texas Citizen
(from the collection of Anita Wood)

ONCE UPON A TIME: ELVIS AND ANITA

Chapter 7

The Draft

Despite Elvis' imminent deployment, the Presleys were determined not to let that spoil the holidays. Christmas was always their favorite time of year — and as 1957 marked their first Christmas at Graceland, they were determined to make it special. The house was decorated beautifully, and the entire family was in a festive mood. It snowed in Memphis that year, so everyone had fun outside building snowmen, riding the sleigh downhill, or simply throwing snowballs at each other. Then Elvis, his parents, Grandma and the rest of the family gathered together with Elvis at the piano, and sang Christmas carols. Momma sat right beside him, as usual, and she still remembers how she nearly melted onto the floor when he looked into her eyes and sang "I'll Be Home for Christmas" and "Blue Christmas." In moments such as those, there was no question about how she felt about him, and she could not help but show it.

It was also Momma's first Christmas with Elvis, of course. He gave her many wonderful presents over the years, which she always appreciated. But what made them truly special, and meaningful, was that Elvis had given them to her.

Now, shopping for Elvis, as you might imagine, was always a challenge — after all, what could you possibly give a man who could have anything he wanted? Momma never bought him clothes, for one, because she didn't think he could fit anything else inside his closets. She does remember giving Elvis a brown sapphire ring that year, plus an inscribed keychain and a watch, while my uncle Andy (Momma's baby brother) bought him a black pair of gloves. Andy used to spend a lot of time hanging out at Graceland with Elvis and the guys, even when Momma wasn't there. She will always remember how special Elvis made Andy feel when he opened his gift: He put those gloves on right away, and didn't take them off the rest of the night.

Christmas at Graceland was a marvelous experience for everyone. The entire house buzzed with joy, and Gladys seemed especially happy. Little did anyone know that this would be her last Christmas with her family.

* * *

Now Elvis was supposed to ship out in January 1958. But because he was in the middle of making *King Creole* when he got his orders — and because of the sheer amount of money that was invested in that movie — the Army gave him a 60-day deferment, until March. Truth be told, that didn't help much, although it did give the Presleys a little more time to prepare themselves for what they were going to do.

A few days after Christmas, Colonel Parker arranged for some beauty queens to come to Graceland to take a picture for the paper publicizing Elvis' draft extension. Naturally, Momma wasn't crazy about that, but as always, she carried on like a good soldier, and hid herself upstairs, away from the camera.

One day near New Year's Eve, Elvis and the guys went out and bought boxes and boxes of Roman candles, so they could shoot them off in the back yard. He and the boys would divide themselves in teams and shoot fireworks at each other. Momma didn't like seeing that, either, especially since no one ever thought about wearing any kind of gear to protect themselves from possible burns. Sure enough, some of the boys did get burned, but they always seemed to laugh it off. It was one of those activities that Elvis enjoyed, because it let him blow off steam. Sometimes, these Roman candle wars would go on for hours.

I mentioned before how it was not always easy for Momma to have to share Elvis with so many other people — and in the weeks before he left, it seemed like everyone in the world wanted to spend as much time with him as she did. One thing she could count on, though, was at the end of the day, when she and Elvis would enjoy some precious alone together before they went to bed. Most nights, Elvis would tell Momma about whatever book he happened to be reading, or they'd talk about what was happening in the world. Sometimes, though, he'd open up to her about his feelings, or recite the words to a song or a poem that was particularly meaningful to him.

One such song was "Satisfied Mind," an old song, written by Red Hayes and Jack Rhodes, that they both liked. Elvis wanted Momma to know the words so that she could always sing along with him. That song must have some special significance to her, because even after all these years, she still has that slip of paper on which she wrote down the lyrics to "Satisfied Mind."

How many times have you heard
someone say. If I had his money
I'd do things my way.
But little they know, that it is so
hard to find - One rich man in
ten with a satisfied mind.
Once I was winning in fortune
and fame. Everything that I
dreamed for to get a start
in life's game. But suddenly
it happened - lost every dime
But I'm richer by far - with
a s. mind.

Money can't buy back. Youth
when you're old. or a friend
when you're lonely or a love
that is grown cold.
The wealthiest person is a
pauper at times. Compared to
the man with a satisfied
mind.

When life has ended, my time
has run out. My friends +
loved ones - I'll leave there
no doubt.

But 1 thing for certain =
When it comes my time -
I'll leave this old world
with a satisfied mind.

Momma says that Elvis truly understood this song, and that the words are oh, so true.

* * *

On January 8, 1958, Elvis celebrated his twenty-third birthday at Graceland with Momma, his parents, all his friends, as well as lots of fans. One of those devoted fans was Gary Pepper, who later became one of Momma's friends. He had cerebral palsy and was confined to a wheelchair, but that didn't stop him from joining in on the fun. He had a huge collection of Elvis memorabilia displayed in his room, which he often showed Momma whenever she visited his family for dinner. She and Gary remained very good friends for many years.

Elvis' family didn't celebrate birthdays too often, but with the Army looming, of course, that year was an exception. Gladys baked him a cake, and everyone gathered in the kitchen to sing "Happy Birthday." The party went on nearly all night, and everyone had a good time.

The next day, Colonel Parker arranged for a little girl, who also happened to be the poster child for the March of Dimes, to have her picture taken with Elvis. He was still sleeping off the party when she got there, but Elvis made it up to her by showering her with attention when he finally did come downstairs, two hours later. (Momma, of course, stayed upstairs with Grandma, so that the press wouldn't know that she'd been there all night.)

A few weeks later, just after Elvis left for New Orleans to start filming *King Creole*, Christian Brothers University, an all-male college in Memphis, asked Momma to run as their homecoming queen, which she agreed to do. She was honored to run, and even more thrilled when she learned that the whole student body had elected her as their queen. It was her first college honor. Not only was Elvis was proud of her, he was particularly happy to see her get so much press coverage without his name even being mentioned. She went to the homecoming dance with a distant cousin, Bruce Harman (not as a date, of course).

Elvis arranged for Momma to take the train down to New Orleans, so they could spend some time together. The first thing she noticed once she arrived was that his sideburns were practically gone. "I felt my character needed a trim, Little," he explained. "Besides, the Army's gonna take 'em off anyway."

Elvis liked filming *King Creole* because it was more of a dramatic role for him. He always preferred playing characters like that over the "silly song parts" he did in so many of his movies. Momma thought he did a good job in that film, while Elvis enjoyed working with Carolyn Jones, Dean Jagger and Walter Matthau. He thought that they all were very talented.

Elvis and Momma talked about the music in that movie, particularly the songs that he had to sing, the messages behind them, and how he chose to sing them. Some songs, of course, he didn't particularly care for, and would not have picked them if it were up to him. (Then again, that was true of every movie he did.) His favorite song in *King Creole* was "Hard Headed Woman," but he also had a lot of fun singing "If You're Looking for Trouble, You've Come to the Right Place." He used to sing that particular line all the time (kiddingly, of course).

While in the Crescent City, Elvis stayed at the Roosevelt Hotel, where he had a bunch of big suites on the top floor that were all connected. He and Momma didn't go out on the town because of safety issues, but they had a good time in his suite. As I'm sure you've gathered by now, Elvis loved to horse around like a little kid, so he and the guys spent a lot of time tossing a shoe around as if it were a football. Being a lady, of course, Momma usually stayed clear of that. One time, however, one of the guys tossed the shoe to her — only it smacked her on the head! She was so mad at herself (embarrassed, really) for not catching that stupid shoe, and she remembers picking it and throwing it back really hard. She also remembers Elvis baby-talking her as if she wasn't hurt (which she wasn't, really, although it *did* sting a lot). She sat out the rest of that game.

Momma and Elvis slept in the same bed while she was there. Each morning one of the guys would knock on the door and say something like, "E, you up?" Momma would then make sure he was awake, then try to go back to sleep while he got dressed and left for the set. By now, of course, "waiting for

Elvis to return" was an all-too familiar scenario. But he always made sure that one of the guys — someone he trusted, of course — stayed with her every day at the hotel. That way, at least Momma would have some company. (She usually spent the day watching movies on television, or catching up on her favorite soaps.)

Some days, Elvis would come home to the hotel and tell her about how a scene went, or how hard the director, Michael Curtiz, made him work. Other days, he just wanted to relax and play around with the rest of the guys.

No one, of course, ever brought up the Army. Instead, they acted as if it was the last thing on their mind, when in fact the opposite was true.

* * *

Back in Memphis, just days before he left for the service, Elvis and Momma were inseparable. He was so loving and affectionate, and yet he was also filled with worry. He knew how fickle the public could be, and that two years was a long time for anyone to be away from the spotlight. Would his fans still listen to his music when he came back?

He also knew how depressed and forlorn his mother was. How would she hold up while he was away?

Most of all, he wondered about his Little. He was so afraid that she would get lonely and want the company of another man. Momma remembers that when he wasn't pacing, he was constantly putting his arms around her and telling her how much he loved her, especially at bedtime. "I'm going to miss you, Little," he said. "But remember that I'll be back, and that I'll call real soon. As soon as I can work it out, I'll get you to come out to wherever I'm stationed."

Of course, as far as Momma was concerned, Elvis had nothing to worry about. He was the one for her, just as she was the one for him. But she certainly understood his anxiety, and did her best to reassure him. She told him how much she loved him, and that she'd wait for him, and that she'd miss him, too. She also told him that she would do whatever she could for his mother.

Now, at this point, no definite plans had been made for either his parents or for Momma to go to where Elvis would be stationed. Besides, they knew that, for the first six or eight weeks, he would be in basic training, which didn't allow for visitors — or so they thought. But we'll get to that soon enough.

In the meantime, Elvis tried to cram in as many activities as he could: He shot pool, watched television, sang and played the piano, rode his motorcycle, rented the fairgrounds (as well as the skating rink and movie theater), and went on long drives with Momma. In fact, for several days in a row, while they were out driving, Elvis kept stopping by car dealerships. Knowing how much he liked cars, she figured he was just looking. But then on March 21, three days before he left for the Army, he found this pink Ford and said, "Little, this looks like you."

Momma couldn't believe it: "Really... for me?!??" She never ever expected him to buy her *a car.*

"But your car is so old, Little," he said. "I don't want you to have any trouble with it while I'm gone."

After all the paperwork was done, Elvis told Momma to follow him out to Graceland so that he could show everybody her new set of wheels. Naturally, the guys were impressed: "Whoo-eee, Anita, you must really rate!"

Vernon said he thought it was a nice car, while Gladys oohed and ahhed over the color. (Some time before, Elvis had bought his mother a pink Cadillac. It was obviously her favorite color.) Momma drove that Ford every day until he gave her another car in 1962.

On March 23, the entire family plus several friends gathered at Graceland to celebrate the night before Elvis left. He made sure it was a joyful occasion with a lot of talking, playing, and singing; Momma doesn't remember going to bed that night. Even Elvis' parents, who were not exactly night owls, stayed up very late. Still, there were moments when Elvis would say, "Man, I'll be gone tomorrow."

One memory Momma will never forget is staying up to watch the sunrise the next morning. It was a beautiful moment, just the two of them together. And yet, knowing what the new day would bring, she also remembers somehow hoping that the night would never end.

Chapter 8

Elvis Rolls Out

When morning came and it was time to go, a caravan of cars accompanied Elvis to the Army depot in Memphis. He was to ride out that day on a bus to Fort Chaffee in Arkansas, before eventually reporting to Fort Hood in Killeen, Texas for basic training.

The Presleys rode in one car; Elvis drove with Momma in the front seat, with his parents and a few others in the back. (Dodger could not come, but Elvis stopped by her room before they left so that he could say goodbye.) Everyone else came in their own cars. It was a somber occasion — almost like a funeral procession, really, although Elvis did try to lighten things up once everyone got there. As you can imagine, the Army officials gave him all kind of paperwork to fill out and sign. Elvis would take a form, read a little bit out loud, then say, "Skip, skip, skip, skip." Sure enough, everyone got a kick out of that.

Still, Elvis was nervous and fidgety; he sat next to Momma for a while, then got up and sat by his parents, then got up and moved around again. Every time he sat near Momma, he looked deeply into her eyes, as if he wanted to tell her something, but couldn't find the words. Momma did her best to assure him with a smile and a knowing look.

In the meantime, Momma tried to keep it together, as did Mrs. Presley. They both knew that it was important that Elvis see them smiling and happy, so he could draw strength from that in the long weeks ahead. Though Gladys came close to crying a few times, she managed to wipe away her tears and maintain a strong front. She always did what was best for Elvis: if she looked upset, he would become upset, too.

But when the time came for him to board that bus, Momma nearly lost it — especially when he looked longingly in her eyes as he turned to say goodbye. "I'll see you soon, Little," he kept saying with a smile. "It won't be too long. I love you. Don't forget, Little — I love you." Then he hugged her and kissed her with all his might before finally getting on the bus.

Like his own momma, Elvis was also trying hard to stay strong and not give in to tears. But that was easier said than done. Like everyone else aboard that bus, he didn't know what the future held, and his whole life seemed in limbo. It's moments like these that remind you that, even considering all he'd accomplished up to that moment, he was only twenty-three years old.

Momma stood arm in arm with Gladys as the bus rolled away. They looked at it in silence for the longest time, even after it faded from view.

"Well, Anita, we're going to miss him," Gladys finally said.

Momma tried to lift her spirits. "It won't be too long," she said.

"Come on now, let's go back home," Gladys said. "I'll fix us something to eat."

Vernon drove them back to Graceland, while Gladys sat next to my mother. Once they were in the car, however, Momma could no longer hide her emotions, and she wept pretty much the whole way back. This time, Gladys comforted her, and eventually she pulled herself together. Like Gladys, Momma knew that she would see him again — she just wasn't sure when.

* * *

Despite the regiments of basic training, Elvis managed to call home just about every day. My mom, of course, was delighted, as was Gladys. Even so, no one expected to see him while he was stationed in Texas. So you can imagine Momma's delight when he called one day and said, "Little, I miss you so much, I want you to come out here. I've got this sergeant friend I met. You can stay with them."

Sure enough, Sergeant William Norwood and his wife, Olley, invited Momma to stay with them and their three children in their home on the base at Fort Hood. Elvis made all the arrangements, and before long she flew out to Texas for a two-week visit.

Knowing that Momma would be there for Elvis made Gladys very happy. "You go out there and make sure my baby's okay," she said before my mother left.

Momma thought the Norwoods were great people. Bill was very nice, while Olley could not have been more accommodating. Whatever Momma needed, she was always there to help. Their mutual love of Elvis bonded them together, but Momma and the Norwoods also became good friends in their own right. In fact, thanks to the Internet, Momma reconnected with Olley and Bill to relive some memories. She has always cherished the time she spent with them, and the kindness they showed her and Elvis.

Still, for Momma, the best part about the trip to Fort Hood was being able to spend time with Elvis without the constant presence of his family or some of "the guys." In some ways, those two weeks were among the best times of their life together.

Momma couldn't see Elvis during the day, of course, but she did see him every night when he came by for supper at the Norwood house. Though he wouldn't eat everything Olley made — she was from Germany, and Elvis was not exactly partial to German dishes — he was always courteous and appreciative. For her part, Olley would sometimes cook foods that she thought Elvis would like, such as black-eyed peas, bacon, and country fried potatoes. One such dish was a simple meal of lettuce, tomatoes and mayonnaise, which Momma had never tried before. She liked it so much, it became one of her favorite meals, even to this day.

After supper, Elvis and Momma would usually watch television for a while with the Norwood family before slipping outside for some quiet time in the backyard. They'd watch the sunset, or gaze out at the stars, in between kissing and hugging. But they'd also talk a lot about the future, and how they'll do all the things that they used to do once Elvis got out of the Army.

Elvis was lonely being away from home, and yet in some ways he seemed more relaxed, and less guarded. He could always be himself with Momma, but now he could do that without any of the pretense that comes with being the King of Rock 'n' Roll. For one, now that he had a regulation Army crew cut, there was no need to dye his hair. So instead of being jet black, his hair was its natural color, light brown (which Momma always preferred, anyway, especially since it made his tanned skin seem even more golden). He also didn't wear lifts in his shoes, like he usually had to. He was just his natural, handsome, charming self, a typical guy that a girl might date and fall in love with.

Of course, if this were a typical relationship, you could say that he and Momma were practically engaged at this time. But because of Colonel Parker, they could never actually say that. In fact, now that Elvis was in the Army, Parker went into overdrive in his efforts to control his image. Besides repeating the edict from on high (about not wanting any stories in the paper about Elvis and Momma), he ordered Momma not to smile if someone were to take their picture. Not only did that go against the grain of her personality, that's just hard to do, *period*.

Still, one night, while gazing at the moon in the backyard of the Norwood home, Elvis told my mother the words she thought she'd never hear: "I'm going to marry you when I get back, Little. I know it's been hard on you, not being able to tell the truth about our relationship — and I appreciate your understanding. But you've proved your loyalty and you have been hanging in there with me and believing in me and being there for me. You always knew that, no matter what, I was coming home to you. You're the one for me."

Momma was so happy that night, for a moment she thought she was dreaming. But it wasn't a dream: Elvis had finally put a timeline on when they would be married. He would repeat this promise many times while he was in Texas, and again throughout the two years he was stationed in Germany. This gave my mother the fortitude to endure the complications of being in love with Elvis Presley.

* * *

One night while Momma was at Fort Hood, one of the officers in Elvis' unit hosted a coffee party at his home, and she and Elvis were asked to attend. Now, Momma had never had a sip of coffee before in her life, but she thought, "If they can drink it, so can I."

Well, she took a drink... and thought it was just awful. In fact, she said it tasted like quinine (or at least, what she imagined quinine must taste like!). Still, being a lady, she wanted to be polite. So she looked around and noticed that some people put cream in their coffee. When no one was watching, she poured some of the coffee out of the cup, added a little cream, and took another sip.

It still tasted terrible.

Then she noticed someone putting sugar in their coffee, so she tried that. She added about four spoonfuls, stirred it into her coffee, and took another sip. That didn't help, either.

Now, at this point, most people wouldn't bother drinking any more; they'd just put the cup down somewhere and go on their merry way. But being a guest in someone's home, Momma didn't want to do that, so she tried her best to finish it. She did, however, make sure that no one around her was watching whenever she took a sip. That way, they couldn't see the ugly face she made every time tasted it!

Still, Elvis couldn't help but notice how giddy she was later that night when he drove her back to the Norwoods. "What's wrong with you, Little, you drunk?" he said with a laugh.

Momma admitted that her head was spinning. "Must be that coffee," she said. "I kept trying to drink it, but I didn't like it. I kept pouring a little of it out and adding something else to it, but it kept tasting awful."

Naturally, Elvis thought that was the funniest thing: "That coffee has made you drunk, Little!" He kept laughing and laughing so hard, his mischievous grin was almost enough to make Momma forget that horrible taste in her mouth. You can believe me when I tell you that she has never tried coffee again!

* * *

Moments like these made it somewhat easier for Elvis to face the uncertain future. So did the times when he spoke to his mother almost every night.

"Things are fine, Momma," he'd say. "Little is right here with me. It's not so bad — I've lost some weight and it's hot, but I'm doing everything that everyone else is doing.

Then he'd ask Gladys about her health. "Are you doing what the doctor says? Are you feeling better?"

Gladys would assure him that she was fine. "That's good, Momma," Elvis would say. "And don't worry — you'll be out here soon, too. I'll make sure of that."

That he did. Once Elvis learned that he would be stationed in Killeen for six months, he arranged for his parents, his grandma, and a few of the guys to come out to Texas. They found a place way out in the country, where no one would find them, and set up a trailer; once Elvis finished basic training, he moved off base and lived in the trailer with his family.

By this time, Momma had to travel to New York every week to fulfill her obligations with AB-PT Productions and ABC Paramount Records. She would spend the week in the Big Apple, then fly back to Texas for weekends. Elvis' room in the trailer had twin beds, so that when Momma stayed over, she'd sleep in one bed, while Elvis slept in the other. Still, as you can imagine, it was pretty tight quarters in that trailer — and it was especially uncomfortable on his mother, given her frail condition. So as soon as he could, Elvis rented a house that had a lot more room for all.

Meanwhile, Gladys cooked Elvis' favorite foods every night: sauerkraut, crisp bacon, sliced tomatoes, Colonial rolls, and Crowder peas. Knowing her son to be a picky eater, she fixed the same thing just about every night. While Elvis spent the day at the base, Gladys would sit and talk to Momma all day, usually about Elvis. As glad as she was to be with her son, she did not want him to go overseas and leave the United States. As she told my mother many times, particularly while they were in Texas, ever since Jesse Garon had died, Gladys became so attached to Elvis because he was now the only child she had — and would ever have. "It's very hard to lose a child," she said. "When you lose one, you put all your attention and everything else on the other one."

Gladys also told my mother how much she wanted Elvis to hurry up and marry her so that they could give her a grandchild. (She wanted to be a grandma in the worst way, but sadly, that was not to be.) She would tell Momma the things that Elvis liked and didn't like, so that she would know how to take proper care of him as his wife someday. "You're just the girl for him, Nita," she'd say. "I know that you'll take care of him, so that he'll always remember his roots and where he came from."

Sometimes Vernon would join them and serenade them with a song called "From a Jack to a King," while Gladys tapped her feet and smiled. As I mentioned before, while Gladys was outspoken and funny, Vernon was more reserved. Yet he seemed to open up more while they were out in Texas — he was certainly much more talkative than Momma had ever seen before. She grew to like him very much.

Still, even though our country was not at war at the time, Gladys worried about Elvis getting hurt. Momma and Vernon did their best to reassure her. Whether her constant anxiety contributed to her illness, no one knows for sure — but Gladys' health in Texas was not great when they lived in the trailer, and it became worse after they moved into the house. Before long, her condition reached the point where Vernon, Gladys and Grandma decided to go back to Memphis so that Gladys could see her own doctor. They hoped that, with rest and medication, she would get well soon. If only that were true.

* * *

About three months later, in June 1958, Elvis came home to Memphis on a two-week furlough. While he was home, he took Momma, his parents, Dodger, and about ten of the guys to the Strand Theater for a special showing of *King Creole*, in advance of its nationwide release on July 2. The event was supposed to be private, and yet somehow word was leaked to the press. Elvis was not happy about that. For that matter, neither was Momma — but when the photographers showed up, she dutifully stepped out of the way. At the end of the night, Elvis let her know how much he appreciated that by whispering some "baby talk" in her ear.

Also during this furlough, Elvis went to Nashville to record some songs. Reporters began calling Momma for interviews and statements — which she always tried to avoid, because it meant that she would have to be evasive about her relationship with Elvis. Even though she was an old pro at this by now, it was never something she enjoyed doing, because it felt like she was lying. Sometimes she'd talk to Elvis about this. He'd tell her that he understood her frustration, and that if it were up to him, he'd tell the whole world just how much she meant to him. But Colonel Parker, of course, would never allow that — and knowing that, Momma would never say or do anything that could hurt Elvis in any way.

In the meantime, Momma continued to pursue opportunities in New York. During her first trip there that year, her manager arranged for some photographers to take pictures upon her arrival at the airport. I am biased, of course, but I think these are some of the best pictures I've ever seen of my mother, because they really show off her beauty. In fact, over the years many people who have seen these photos immediately compare her to Marilyn Monroe. Even my own children have thought that! One time, when we were at a restaurant, they noticed some pictures of Marilyn Monroe on the wall. They immediately asked me if that was their mamaw.

June 1958 was also the month in which Momma recorded her first single ABC Paramount Records: "I'm Liking This," with a cover of "Crying in the Chapel" on the B side. Don Costa, who was well known in the music industry, arranged and conducted that record; he was working for ABC Paramount at the time and picked out both songs for Momma. She remembers how he kept coaching her to sing "I'm Liking This" so that it was "breathy." The end result was a song that many believe to be incredibly sexy — which is funny, considering how innocent my mother was about those things at the time. She wasn't trying to convey anything; she was just singing it as best she could, the way Don Costa wanted it.

Nevertheless, many stations refused to play "I'm Liking This" because they thought it was too suggestive. Even Elvis believed it was over the top: "It's a pretty song, Little, and you sound good, but it's a little too risqué for you — too modern."

As for "Crying in the Chapel," Costa told Momma to sing it in whatever way she wanted. Not surprisingly, Elvis liked this song much better. In fact, he would often play it on the piano at Graceland and have her sing it, while he did harmony.

A few years later, in 1960, Elvis himself recorded a cover of "Crying in the Chapel," although the record was not released until 1965. As Casey Kasem might put it, it eventually made its way all the way up to No. 3 on the Billboard charts.

Shortly after cutting her record, Momma made her first appearance on *The Jack Paar Tonight Show.* Paar not only found her very charming, but invited her back to sing on the show. In addition, Momma's contract also had her appear every week on *The Andy Williams Show,* which ran for thirteen weeks that summer on ABC. Dick Van Dyke was also a regular on that show. Andy Williams was a nice person as far as my mother could tell, but he was also quiet and somewhat distant. He would greet her and talk to her when he needed to, but beyond that he kept to himself. Dick Van Dyke, on the other hand, was always outgoing, friendly, funny and polite. Momma talked to him every time they were on the set together.

Ironically, even though she had just released a record, Momma did not sing at all during the first six weeks she appeared on the Williams show. Instead, they made her into a sort of "mystery guest," where she would walk across the set, wearing some kind of costume, smile at the camera, then quietly walk off stage.

Though some thought she was getting the brush-off, Elvis was always positive. "That's just the way these shows work, Little," he said. "As long as Andy Williams was on there, they don't care about anybody else." Elvis wasn't always able to tune in, but if he did happen to see her on the show, he always called her to say, "You did good."

Also that summer, my grandmother flew to New York so that Momma would have some company. (That made Elvis very happy, as he did not want his Little to be alone in the big city.) They stayed together in Momma's room at the Hotel Edison. A few weeks later, Momma's father, along with her three brothers, drove up to New York to join them for a couple of weeks (that served as the family vacation). While Momma tended to her engagements, the rest of them shopped, walked around, did some sightseeing, as well as visited one of Mamaw's brothers in Long Island (where he lived with his wife).

Also while she was in New York, Momma attended the Burt Lane Theater Workshop, where she learned about drama and was also coached on how to play different characters. The teacher there said that to be a good actress, one had to have experienced, to some degree, what the character was portraying.

"If that's what it takes," Momma thought to herself, "I'll never be a good actress," because she knew there was so much in her life that she had not yet experienced.

* * *

Every week that summer, after taping *The Andy Williams Show* on Thursday, Momma would fly to Fort Worth for the weekend, where one of the guys (usually Lamar Fike) would pick her up at the airport. Sometimes, when Elvis had time off, the two of them would just get in his convertible and start driving without a specific destination; every once in a while, they'd stay in a motel and go swimming.

One time, she and the gang drove off to some town where Elvis had a meeting with Colonel Parker. While Elvis met with Parker, Momma and the guys went to the hotel restaurant, where she ordered a huge tray of boiled shrimp cocktail. That was a real treat for her because, considering how much Elvis hated fish, she didn't get to eat it that often. As a matter of fact, when Elvis met them at the restaurant after finishing his meeting, he refused to join them at the table until all the shrimp was gone.

On another such excursion, Elvis drove Momma to Waco, where he introduced her to his friend Eddie Fadal. Elvis thought Eddie was a good guy, and he liked spending time with his family. Eddie was a huge fan; he took pictures of Elvis and recorded him with video and audio. Momma has a video that someone gave her that includes footage from Eddie's house. She wore a simple, straight, hot pink dress that day, which her mother had made for her, and which Elvis liked very much. (In that video, Elvis plays around kissing Momma on the check every so often, but at one point he kisses her hot and heavy!)

My mom also has heard some of the audio recordings that Eddie made, including one in which she sings "I Can't Help It If I'm Still In Love With You," with Elvis singing back-up. It's hard to imagine Elvis backing up anyone, but when it came to his Little, as I say, one of the things he loved to do was play the piano and sing harmony with her.

Eddie made Elvis feel at home, and Elvis certainly did. One time he and the guys decided to watch a movie, while Momma played with Eddie's little girl. To this day Momma doesn't know what they were watching, but it must not have been something nice — Elvis would not let her in the room until it was over.

One weekend, a few days before her twentieth birthday (May 27, 1958), Momma and Elvis celebrated the occasion at Eddie's house with a birthday cake, and Elvis singing and playing "Happy, Happy Birthday, Baby" over and over again. He even slow-danced with her once when she asked him to, which was something he never did, because, as I say, he didn't think he was a particularly good dancer. But he was in such high spirits that day, it didn't matter!

Thursday, August 14, 1958 was supposed to be another big day in my mother's life. That night, she was scheduled to sing for the first time on *The Andy Williams Show*. Interestingly enough, instead of letting her perform one of the songs from her record, she was told to sing an old standard, "You Made Me Love You." Momma remembers belting it out in her usual style during rehearsal. But then someone told her to make the arrangement softer and more subdued, which did not suit my mother's vocal abilities in the slightest.

In any event, Momma was asleep in her hotel room early that morning when she and Mamaw were jolted awake by the phone. It was Elvis calling, and he did not have good news. In fact, when my mother looks back on it now, this was the day when everything changed, beginning with that fateful call.

?ampus Queen

Homecoming Queen of Christian Brothers College
(from the collection of Anita Wood)

Anita with some students at CBC
(*from the collection of Anita Wood*)

Elvis and Anita looking for cars right before he bought her first car.
(Courtesy of Memphis Press-Scimitar)

Elvis looking over his Army papers.
(Courtesy of Brian Petersen)

Elvis making everyone laugh by saying "Skip…Skip…Skip"
(Courtesy of Brian Petersen)

Elvis and Anita looking into each other's eyes while waiting.
(From the collection of Russ Howe)

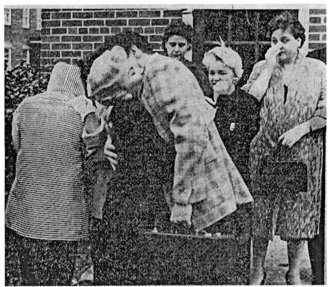

The final hug goodbye. *(Courtesy of Memphis Press-Scimitar)*

Anita looking anguished as Elvis boards the bus.
(Courtesy of Brian Petersen)

Posing on the runway after returning from New York.
(from the collection of Anita Wood)

Sprucing up for the camera in New York.
(From the collection of Anita Wood)

Painting the set on *The Andy Williams Show*. *(Courtesy of Memphis Press-Scimitar Morgue Files/Special Collections, University of Memphis Libraries)*

Elvis and Anita at Eddie Fadal's house. *(From the collection of Janice Fadal)*

With Eddie and his wife. *(From the collection of Janice Fadal)*

A picture that Elvis gave Anita in Texas with a telephone number where he could be reached in Kileen. *(From the collection of Anita Wood)*

Video captures of Anita and Elvis smooching,
from home movies taken at Eddie Fadal's house.
(From the collection of Janice Fadal)

ANITA WOOD

Autographed photo *(From the collection of Janice Fadal)*

Chapter 9

Precious Memories

My grandmother knew something was wrong the minute she answered the phone in Momma's room. Elvis didn't sound like his usual self. In fact, he could barely speak at all.

"What's wrong, Elvis?" Momma asked.

He was calling from Memphis Hospital and spoke with a heavy heart. "She's gone, Little," he said. "She's gone."

The Army granted Elvis emergency leave the day before, when he learned that his mother had become gravely ill. He arrived at the hospital in time to see her, then decided to go home to Graceland and rest before returning in the morning. He was away from her for just a few short hours, but in that window of time Gladys Presley passed away. She was forty-six years old.

"I want you to come home right now," Elvis said. He was weeping inconsolably.

If she could, my mom would have climbed through the phone lines to put her arms around him. "I have to do the show this afternoon," she said. "But I will be there as soon as I can."

Momma did her best to get through the taping of *The Andy Williams Show*, but her mind was clearly elsewhere. All she could do was think of Elvis and Vernon; what were they going to do now that Gladys was gone?

Elvis arranged for Momma to fly to Memphis right after her performance. Lamar Fike was waiting for her at the airport, driving a white limousine. In the meantime, because Elvis wanted his mother brought out to Graceland as soon as possible, he asked the funeral home to do a rush job, so to speak. They not only accommodated his request, but did a remarkable job preparing the body for viewing in just a few hours. She was lying in repose in the music room at Graceland when Momma and Lamar arrived.

Elvis and his daddy were sitting on the front steps by the lions when Lamar pulled up beside them. When Momma got out of the car, she still had her heavy stage makeup on, plus the gown, false eyelashes and ponytail hair extension she wore for the Williams show — she was so anxious to fly back home, she didn't even think of changing.

Elvis grabbed her and clung to her tightly as he began to weep. "I'm so glad you're here, Little," he said. "Come on inside. I want you to see Momma."

My mother hesitated. She had never seen a body in a casket before, much less someone she loved. "Oh, I don't think I can, Elvis," she said. "I just don't think I can."

"Please, Little," he said. "She loved you, and I want you to go inside. It's the last time you'll be able to see her."

So Elvis took Momma by the hand and led her into the music room, where Gladys was laid in a beautiful ornate casket. She was dressed in a simple yet pretty house dress; her fingernails were painted pink, and her feet were bare.

Elvis had the funeral parlor raise up the end of the casket so that her entire body was viewable. Though the casket was left open for viewing, the body was protected by a glass top. (Sometime later, my mother would learn this was to keep Elvis from petting and touching his mother constantly.)

"Look at her little sooties," Elvis said, pointing to his mother's feet. "See those little sooties, and see those little toes. That's her, Little. That's Momma right there."

It was a poignant moment. They stood there and cried and quietly talked as other people paid their respects.

After a while, Momma tried to ease her way out of the room, but Elvis wouldn't let her leave. "Come here beside me, Little," he said. "She loved you, Little."

"I know," Momma said. "I loved her, too." She did everything she could to be strong for Elvis, the way Gladys would have wanted her to be. But it was extremely hard, not to mention uncomfortable, whenever he started "baby talking" to his mother, or patting the glass over her body.

At one point, however, she asked if he wouldn't mind if she went upstairs so that she could change her clothes and get rid of the heavy stage makeup. "Okay, Little," said Elvis. "You go check on Dodger, too."

"I will," she assured him. "I'll be right back."

As she made her way upstairs, Momma noticed for the first time just how many people were in the house. The place was cram-packed with family and friends, but there were just as many faces that she had never seen before. She had no idea what they were doing there, or if they had any connection to the family. There was plenty of food, or course, though Elvis himself had little to eat.

Because there were so many people in the house, however, they did not want to risk anyone telling the press about Momma and Elvis sleeping in the same bed. So that night she slept with Grandma, while Elvis slept with some of his male cousins. Dr. Nacompliss, the family doctor, gave him and his father some sedatives to help them deal with the shock.

The funeral was the next day. Reverend James Hamill, the pastor at the Assembly of God Church in Memphis, where Elvis worshiped as a boy, presided. Elvis, his dad and his grandma sat in the front row; Momma sat right behind them, along with Patsy and the other members of the family. The

Blackwood Brothers sang "Rock of Ages," "In the Garden," "I am Redeemed," and "Precious Memories." Elvis cried throughout the entire service, but when they sang "Precious Memories" he lost it completely — that song was one that he and his mother particularly loved.

Momma leaned over, put her hand on his shoulder and tried her best to console him. "What am I gonna do, Little?" Elvis said. "How will I make it without her?"

* * *

The next few days were a blur. There were so many people milling about the house, while Elvis himself was in a daze. He was clearly distraught over the loss of his mother, and yet he didn't want to talk about it. If someone mentioned the funeral, or anything else that reminded him of Gladys, he would turn on the television and look for the news, or an old movie, or anything that might distract him. Sometimes he and Momma would sit and talk around the kitchen counter, or walk around the yard, or head up to his office, just to get away. Then, when he got tired of being numb, he'd take a sedative and lie down. Momma was happy to see him rest, because that allowed some relief from all that stress and agony.

Momma sat and talked with Dodger while Elvis slept. Like everyone else, Grandma was worried about Vernon and Elvis, so she took matters in her own hands. Whereas she used to spend most of the day in her room, she started coming downstairs more often, sometimes to cook some of their favorite foods, but mostly just to be there for them. In a way, you might say it was as though she'd come out of retirement.

One day, shortly after the funeral, Dixie Locke, one of Elvis' former girlfriends, came by to pay her respects. Elvis asked if he could see her alone, and my mother gladly obliged. She knew that Dixie had known Gladys, and besides, in moments such as these, it's good to be able to spend time with lost loved ones and relive a few memories.

Those first few days after Gladys died were among the most painful in Elvis' life. It was so hard for him to fathom a world without her in it, and even more difficult to realize that soon he would have to leave again and resume his military duties. Momma remembers that he hugged her just about every chance he could.

In a way, though, it was probably a blessing that Elvis had to return to Fort Hood — at the very least, his service in the Army got him out of the house and back on a daily regiment of activities. Had he been allowed to remain at Graceland, there is no telling what he would have spiraled into right then and there.

Duty called for Momma as well. Knowing how fragile Elvis was, the last thing she wanted to do was leave his side. But as they say in the entertainment business, "The show must go on," and contractual obligations required her to return to New York. She continued, however, to fly down to Texas every weekend.

She remembers her first trip back down there. By the time she arrived in Killeen, the house Elvis had rented was completely out of control. There were people everywhere, in every room — people that she had never seen before. Elvis had always made his home welcome to fans, but this was something else. These weren't fan club presidents, or people he had to come to know, but rather complete strangers. Guys were making out with girls at random. It was total chaos.

Meanwhile, Elvis was alone at the piano, oblivious to it all. *"What is going on here?"* Momma thought to herself as she sat down next to him. *"Who are all these strange people?!?"*

Strange, how grief affects us in different ways. Elvis and his father were so deep in mourning, they didn't care what was going on around them. Sometimes it would get to him — but even so, the only thing Elvis would do was jump in the car with Momma and start driving around, with no particular destination in mind.

All Dodger could do was shake her head. "This is the biggest mess I've ever seen," she said. "I don't know what to do!"

* * *

August became September... and as the song goes, the days dwindled down to a precious few before September 20, when Elvis was scheduled to ship out to Germany. The night before he left was as solemn and emotional as that night in Memphis six months before, when he boarded the bus for basic training. Only difference was, the train for Germany didn't leave until seven o'clock that evening. This made for a long, drawn out, sad, very difficult and often intense goodbye.

All summer long, Elvis had promised Momma that she would come with him, along with his father and grandma. He repeated that promise that night: "I can't go for that long without you, Little. You're coming to Germany. I'll make plans. As soon as I leave, I want you to go to your mother's house and start working on getting your passport, so you'll be ready to come when I get situated over there. When I get a place, I'll call you and you'll just come over there."

So that's exactly what Momma did. She got her shots, took care of her passport papers, and waited. It would be a long wait.

In the meantime, she and Elvis talked all night and pledged their love to one another, vowing that their love would never die and that no distance could keep them apart. "No matter what you see in the paper, or hear, just know how much I love you," Elvis told her. "That is the real truth."

It was not an easy separation, but Elvis gave Momma something to remember him by: a built-up ring that had grooves with a big diamond in the middle and two rows of diamonds on the sides. Elvis used to wear it all the time on his pinky finger; Momma wore it on a chain around her neck, and close to her heart, every day while he was in Germany. She held on to that ring for a while even after they broke up in 1962. (Eventually, before she married my father, she passed it on to her good friend Gary Pepper, a devoted Elvis fan. Gary can be seen wearing that ring in one of Momma's wedding pictures.)

On September 20, 1958, Elvis boarded the train that left Fort Hood, en route to Germany. That day, the *New York Journal American* ran a front page picture of Elvis and Momma with the headline GI AND THE GIRL HE LEFT BEHIND.

Ironically, when Elvis left Germany two years later, the media would use the same headline — only this time, it would refer to a young girl he'd met overseas named Priscilla Beaulieu. When asked about it by the press, Elvis denied having any serious relationship with Priscilla other than a friendship... just as he had done with my mom.

ONCE UPON A TIME: ELVIS AND ANITA

Chapter 10

5,000 Miles Away

Almost immediately the press called Momma for interviews or statements about Elvis. She was well rehearsed on what to say and not say, and she always played down their relationship whenever someone asked. That wasn't easy, considering how she really felt — and every once in a while, she'd let the truth come out, at least a little. But whenever that happened, she always quickly covered herself by changing the subject.

Of course, the press reported Elvis' every move, from his Army duties to the pretty frauleins who always seemed to accompany him — all of which Momma followed in the papers. You can imagine how hard that was for her, too.

Fortunately for Momma, she didn't have time to become too sad or depressed. After renewing her contract (with a raise in salary), Henry Plitt, her manager with Paramount Gulf Theatres, kept her busy with a schedule that included another appearance in New York on *The Jack Paar Tonight Show* (where Momma wowed the studio audience with her rendition of "Again"), as well as appearances on local television programs in Memphis and other parts of the country. She also had fun donning a sexy maid's uniform as part of a photo shoot for a Holiday Inn advertisement. Mr. Plitt even set up a dinner date with George DeWitt, the nationally known comedian, singer, and friend of Frank Sinatra, who opened for Ole Blue Eyes in New York and Atlantic City.

Of course, Momma told Elvis about this, and assured him that there was nothing going on between them — it was only for publicity's sake. While Elvis wasn't happy to hear that, he really couldn't say too much, because he himself had used that same excuse with Momma so many times before, whenever she saw photographs of him in the arms of some beauty queen: "Oh, Little, that's just publicity."

Whether Elvis was being truthful when he used that excuse, I don't know. But in Momma's case, she was.

Once he set up his private residence, Elvis tried to reach Momma at Graceland. By this time, however, two weeks had passed. Momma felt she had no reason to stay in Memphis while Elvis was overseas, so she decided to move in with her parents in Jackson, Tennessee. Unfortunately, because of her busy schedule, she didn't have a chance to tell him that she had moved (as he had asked her to do). So when Elvis called, obviously, Momma wasn't there. Fortunately, he reached her friend Mrs. Davidson and gave her his number in

Germany. Though Momma was sad that she'd missed his call, she was also excited because she knew that Elvis was okay.

Momma returned the call the next day, and when Elvis answered she nearly jumped out of her skin. His voice sounded funny, like he was talking in a barrel, but it was Elvis and she was overjoyed.

"How're you doing over there?" she asked.

"Oh, fine," said Elvis. "Folks are friendly enough, Little, 'cept that nobody speaks any English. I don't like it when people talk around me and I don't know what they are saying."

"You miss home?" said Momma.

"Yes, I do," said Elvis. "I talked to Daddy and I talked to Dodger last night, and I know they're both getting mighty lonesome. You got your passport yet?"

"I'm working on it."

"That's good, Little. You know I'm trying to get you here just as soon as I can."

Then he asked Momma to do him a favor. "I want you to start writing me. I'm gonna give you my address, so that your letters will always go straight to me."

"All right," said Momma. "Will you write me back?

He hesitated for a moment. "I don't know, Little... you know I'm not one for writing letters. But I will call you every week, I promise."

True to his word, Elvis called Momma once a week, and sometimes more than that. He was afraid that she might find someone else while he was gone, so he always peppered his calls with how much he loved her, missed her, and wanted to be back home.

One night, when Elvis called, Momma was bursting with good news. "I finally got my picture and papers ready for my passport!" she squealed.

Much to her surprise, however, Elvis grew silent. "I'm sorry to have to tell you this," he finally said, "but Colonel Parker said no."

Needless to say, Momma's heart sank. "I don't understand... You know how much I want to see you. I got all my shots and everything."

"I'm so sorry, Little," said Elvis. "I want you to come so bad."

He told Momma that, according to the Colonel, if word got around that she was coming to Germany, the press would have them engaged or married — and that would be bad for Elvis' public image. "Son, you don't need anything like that right now," Parker told Elvis. "You need to be absolutely free for when you come back home and resume your career."

Again Elvis apologized; he seemed as upset about it as Momma was. "But he's my manager, Little, I have to do what he says about my career... and he says you coming here will ruin it."

* * *

After this conversation, Elvis must have decided that if he couldn't bring Momma to Germany, he would have to start writing her. He sent her pictures, postcards, and Valentines cards. And though he didn't like writing letters, he also wrote my Momma three long, multi-page, heartfelt love letters in which he poured out his feelings and reinforced many of the things he'd been saying on the phone.

The first letter from Elvis was on stationery from the Hotel Grunewald:

Dear Little Bitty,

      For the first time in a hundred years I am writing a letter. You can see why I don't like to write. The reason being I can't write worth a ???! I just thought of so many things I wanted to say to you and I couldn't say them on the phone. You'll never know how much I miss you baby and how much I want to pet you and call you "Widdle Bitty." Your little picture is by my bed and every night before I go to sleep I always say "goodnight little Pee Pee." The people over here are very nice and friendly although they are living about 30 years behind us. Don't quote me. I haven't dated a single girl since I have been here, the reason being I don't have time and every time I get out of the hotel I get mobbed. Also I haven't seen a girl yet that could speak English. You say Hello to one and she says "Luben Slich Ein E P skip skip skip VON HEIMER Bull Shit!" I want to explain something to you and you have got to trust me and believe me because I am very serious when I say it. I will tell you this much. I have never and never will again love any one like I love you sweetheart. Also I guarantee that when I marry it will be Miss "Little Wood Presley." There is a lot you have to understand though only God knows when the time will be right. So you have got to consider this and love me, trust me and keep yourself clean and wholesome because that is the one big thing that can determine our lives and happiness together. If you believe me and trust me you will wait for me and our future will be filled with happiness. With God's help it will work itself out and you will understand and be patient. I worked so hard to build up my career and everything and if you truly love me you would not want anything to happen to it and cause me to be unhappy. No matter what I am doing, whether it is the army, making movies, traveling or singing I will be thinking of the time when we have our first "Little Elvis Presley." So have this in mind and don't get discouraged and lonely. Just remember there is a guy that loves you with all his heart and wants to marry you. One more thing honey for goodness sake please don't let anyone read this and don't say a word about this letter to anyone. You know how I hate that so be careful baby. If you love me and you are sincere you wouldn't want to let anyone know our intimate secrets. I better go for now love, so be happy and remember down in your little heart that I love you, love you, love you. Keep writing.

Yours Alone and Forever
E. P.

P. S. I Love You

Now I ask you, who could dispute that Elvis loved my mom after reading that? Most girls I know would die to receive a letter like that!

Momma cherishes this letter to this day. It's one thing to have someone say I Love You, but it's totally different to have it expressed in words that you can hold on to and read over and over again. Though circumstances forced them to keep their relationship secret, at least Momma knew just how much she meant to him — and she believed that, once Elvis came home, it wouldn't be long before the rest of the world would finally know how much he loved her, too.

* * *

Elvis continued to call Momma at every opportunity. Because of his schedule, there was no set pattern to when he'd call — sometimes it was early morning, sometimes late at night. Good thing Momma was a light sleeper, because she woke up easily to answer the phone. On those occasions when Momma was out of town for a singing engagement, Elvis would talk to my grandmother and find out how to reach her.

Momma also wrote Elvis many letters, telling him everything that was going on in her life while asking what was happening with him. Sometimes, the press reports of all the girls he was supposedly seeing would be too much for her, and she'd let her frustrations show. Elvis, of course, denied that anything was going on, and did his best to reassure her. Still, it was another indication that the next eighteen months were going to be long and hard.

One time, Elvis called Momma and said, "Get some paper, Little. I have a song I want you to write down." This was not unusual; many times Elvis would read something, or hear a poem or a song, and want her to write down the words so she could be thinking about the same things he was. He really had a photographic memory. On this occasion, he wanted to share with her a song by Marty Robbins called "Tomorrow You'll Be Gone." When he finished reciting, Elvis said, "Did you write that down, Little?"

"Yes, I did," said Momma. "That's good. I want you to read that sad song and think on it."

Momma not only thought on those words while Elvis was away, she still has the sheet of paper on which she wrote them.

* * *

Meantime, Momma continued to travel to different cities across the country for performances, always making sure to let her parents know how to reach her whenever Elvis called. She spent a week in New Orleans performing two shows a night at the famous Swan Room at the Hotel Monteleone, where she was billed as "Anita Wood, Paramount's Newest Star."

During this time, Momma learned that Elvis had written her another letter — and as you can imagine, she could not wait to get home to read it!

Once again Elvis poured out his heart to her. Through these letters we really do get a window into their relationship:

My Dearest Little Darling,

I just received your letters and I can judge by the last 3 that you are a little disappointed. Well I can't blame you, especially since all that mess was written about "little puppy" and all that "horse shit." Well I don't know where they get the information but the girl they speak of was a photographer's model and she was brought over by some news man. The first week I was here. I have seen her one time since then. She doesn't speak a word of English and I have not been dating her and I did not say all that stuff about seeing her 4 or five times and I have not tried to keep anything from you. You see that was really played up big because the paper figured it was good for German, American relationship. Do you understand? But don't you dare ever mention it to a soul because if you do I am finished in Germany. Just keep it inside of you and regardless of what you read or what obstacles come up in our way please remember that I am yours my darling, yours, yours, yours, yours, yours. No one will ever take the place of "My Little" in my life. Baby you will never know how lonesome and miserable I am. I will be so thankful to God when once again I am free, free to return back to singing, making movies and above all returning to your little arms and lips. Every night I lay in my bunk I see your little eyes

129

and your little nose and it's almost like you are here, like you are pressed up close to me. I can feel your little hair on the side of my face and sometimes I get so excited and want you so bad I start sweating.

"WOW"

"Well so much for that"

Listen my Love never doubt my love for you always trust me and believe me when I say that I love you. It sure is going to be a blue Christmas this year. But in 15 short months it'll be over and as General MacArthur said, "I shall return." Have a merry Christmas Darling and remember there is a lonely little boy 5000 miles away that's counting the hours till he returns to your arms. If you get a chance try to locate a record called "Soldier Boy." Play it and think of me. By the way our song from now on is "Love me forever" by Tommy Edwards. Every night I play it just for you. Always loving and wanting you.

"Yours alone darling"

Elvis Presley

P. S. No one ever reads this OK!

Later that day, Momma went to the record store and bought those two songs. She not only thought of Elvis when she played "Soldier Boy," but told him the next time he called that the lyrics captured exactly how she felt about him. Elvis himself later recorded this song in 1960.

Prior to this letter, Elvis and Momma's song had been "I Can't Help It If I'm Still In Love with You." By now, though, it was clear to Momma that "Please Love Me Forever" spoke of how afraid Elvis was that she would find another man while he was away — no matter how many times she assured him otherwise.

"Please Love Me Forever" continued to be their song after Elvis came back from Germany. They both thought it was beautiful, and he and Momma sang it together many, many times while he played it on the piano:

* * *

Momma tried to be jovial when the holidays came, but it was hard without Elvis around. Fortunately, he arranged for the special delivery of a delightful Christmas present: a soft, tiny, fluffy white French poodle, which Momma soon named "Little," because he really was no bigger than the length of her hand. Momma gushed with joy about the puppy when Elvis called, and he told her to "snuggle up to that little bitty thing" until he got back home.

By January 1959, Momma had long settled into the routine of communicating with Elvis at least once a week by phone, and through cards and letters every other week. Elvis sent her lots of photos, including one of him in a convertible with "I love you love you love you, love you little" written on the back, and another in which he wore a turban, a long robe and sunglasses. Big goofy kid that he was, he couldn't resist drawing a mustache and goatee on himself! (On the front of the photo, he wrote "Love you always From 'The Thing,'" while the back said "To Little with all my love, E. P. Elvis Presley.") He also sent her a Valentines card, a picture of him in his Army uniform, another picture from an earlier time in his life, and a postcard of the Hotel Grunewald (where he drew a circle around the top floor and wrote, "This is where we live... The whole top floor!").

The year would be another long one, but again Momma kept busy. In early January, she was invited to audition for a small role in the Broadway production of Tennessee Williams' *Sweet Bird of Youth* that was scheduled to open in March. Elia Kazan was the director, and he told Momma that he'd listened to her record and liked her voice. All she had to do was walk out on the stage and let a group of men see her. The audition seemed to go well, because Momma got a call back to meet Kazan in his office.

To Momma's horror, however, it soon became apparent that Kazan wanted her to go to bed with him. "If you want to make it in this business," he said, "that's what you'll have to do."

But, to Kazan's surprise, Momma said no. From that moment on, she decided that she wanted nothing more to do with acting. She was tired of Hollywood, tired of New York, tired of the entertainment industry in general. All she really wanted to do was sing or maybe DJ again.

Also in January 1959, Momma was the opening act for Buddy Hackett at the Black Orchid nightclub in Chicago. It was an eighteen-night run, two shows a night, and she performed a few songs during each set. Momma liked Buddy very much; she told me that, in some ways, he reminded her of her father. They went out to eat together all the time, and as he got to know her better, Buddy said, "You're too nice a girl for this kind of business, Anita. You need to go home and get yourself married."

If only Buddy knew, that's exactly what she wanted to do. But the man she loved wasn't ready to marry her.

Also while performing at The Black Orchid, Momma met Sammy Davis, Jr. She knew that Elvis knew him, and Sammy knew that she was Elvis' girl. But that didn't stop Sammy from sending her roses, with cute messages like "You ain't nothing but a hound dog" scribbled on the card. That made Momma a little uncomfortable — partly because she didn't think it was proper for someone to send flowers to the girlfriend of a friend, but mostly because she knew how insane Elvis would become if he were to find out.

Personally, I think it was a nice gesture, and I don't believe Sammy meant anything else by it. Still, I understand how Momma felt. She was so close to Elvis, she practically programmed herself not to show interest in any of the men around her. Otherwise, it would be as if she were being disloyal to him.

During this engagement in Chicago, my father, Johnny Brewer, saw Momma for the second time — only this time, he got to see her perform. He was in town to play in the College All-Star Football Game (by that time, he'd already been drafted by the Cleveland Browns of the NFL). One of Daddy's fellow All-Stars lived in the area and invited him out for a night on the town. Daddy sat at a table with Buddy Hackett, as a matter of fact, as well as some guy who was involved with *Playboy*. Once again, Daddy thought Momma was beautiful, although he did not recognize her as the girl he'd seen before with Elvis. Her hair had grown out, plus she was much more outgoing on stage, engaging the audience with her eyes while charming them with her voice. It was quite a contrast from that night in Memphis, where he saw her at the theater with Elvis. That night, you'll recall, Momma gazed her eyes only at Elvis, never looking to the right or left.

* * *

Though Momma continued to sing over the next months, she also took a job as a disc jockey with WHHM in Memphis. Her show ran Monday through Friday, 4:30pm to 6:00pm, and the station gave her full latitude.

One day in October, Elvis surprised Momma by phoning her at the station with exciting news: he'll be coming home around March 3. But it was also around this time that pictures of him with a young girl named Priscilla began surfacing in the papers. Momma didn't like that at all, and she let Elvis know it. Though he again said that "It's all for publicity, nothing's going on," it was getting harder for her to believe that.

A few weeks later, Elvis wrote Momma another lengthy letter:

My Dearest Darling "<u>Little</u>,"
Well here I am back out in the field for 30 days again and believe me it's miserable. There is only one consolation, and that is the fact that it's almost over, and I will come home to my career, friends, and most of all you my darling, Anita there are many things I can't tell you over the phone so I will try to tell you now. First of all I don't really know how you feel about me now because after all 2 years is a long time in a young girl's life. But I want you to know that in spite of our being apart I have developed a love for you that cannot be equaled or surpassed by anyone. My every thought is you my darling, every song I hear, every sunset reminds me of the happy and wonderful times we've spent together. I tell you this because I want you to know my feeling toward you have not changed, but instead has grown stronger than I ever thought it could. I have hurt you sometimes because I was mad at some of the things you did or I thought you did, but every time these things happened I thought that maybe you only liked me for what I am, and didn't really love me for myself. These things happen in life baby, misunderstandings, heartbreaks and loneliness, but the fact remains, if it's really love Anita, if we really love each other it will last, and these things will be something of the past, although things will come up in the future that will hurt us both. They are to be expected. I have had feelings that in the last few months something has happened as far as you're concerned, not only because you haven't written but by the sound of your voice when I talk to you. The warmth and love seems to have dimmed. It may be my imagination but you seem as though you have something to tell me but yet you're not sure. I hope I'm wrong. You know after going through what I have in the last 18 months you sometimes wonder if anyone really cares. Please believe me when I tell you it's you and only you my darling. But I think that you will keep your word, and tell me if you had grown to care for someone else and vice versa. I have been sleeping out on the ground, and I have a fever and tonsillitis again. I am listening to the radio and all the guys are sitting around with sad looks on their faces. Do you remember when you used to bounce for me and I would laugh so hard? Darling I pray that you haven't let your loneliness, passions, and desires make you do something that would hurt me. If you have it is better you tell me now. I can't believe you have or would. Well we are all counting

the days until we come home. The reason I didn't want you there on the first night because in spite of the fact that I love my friends and relatives, when we first lay eyes on each other we will cling to each other like a vine. So I think some other people might get their feelings hurt. So please understand honey. You have surprised me at how understanding you are. So darling if you still feel the same and if you love me and me alone we will have a great life together even though you hear things and read things. Just think as you said, everyone knows how I feel about you. I can't explain to you how I crave you and desire your lips and your body under me darling. I can feel it now. The things we did and the desire we had for each other's body!!! Remember darling, true love hold its laurels through the ages no matter how loud the clamor of denial. That which deserves to live-lives.

> Yours Alone,
> E P

Come Christmastime, Elvis again arranged for special delivery of Momma's present. This time, he gave her a guitar that was inscribed "To Little, From EP" on the front, plus a fancy sound system and just about every guitar accoutrement you can think of. When he returned from Germany, Elvis not only played many songs for Momma on that guitar, but taught her how to play it, just like he'd taught her to play the piano. (In case you're wondering... no, Momma no longer has that guitar. She gave it away many years ago, as a wedding gift to a friend of hers who was a huge Elvis fan.)

Meanwhile, Elvis continued to call her every week, as well as send her pictures (and, of course, a Valentines card). Finally, March arrived. After eighteen long months, he was returning home to Momma. She could hardly wait.

ONCE UPON A TIME: ELVIS AND ANITA

(The first letter Elvis sent Anita from Germany.)

HOTEL GRUNEWALD
BAD NAUHEIM
TELEFON 2230

BAD NAUHEIM, DEN
TERRASSENSTRASSE 10

Dear little Bitsy,

For the first time in a hundred years I am writing a letter. you can see why I don't like to write the reason being I can't write with a _____! I just thought of so many things I wanted to say to you and I couldn't say them on the phone. you'll never know how much I miss you baby, and how much I want to pet you and call you widdle oolsy". your little picture is by my bed and every night before I go to sleep I always say "goodnight little Lee Pee". The people over here are very nice and friendly although they are living about 30 years behind us. Don't quote me. I haven't dated a single girl since I have been here. The reason being I don't have time, everytime I get out of the hotel I get mobbed also I haven't seen a girl yet that could speak English. you say Hello to one and she says "Iuben Slich Ein Ep Step Step Step VON HEIMER Ball SHIT". I want to explain something to you and you have got to trust me and believe me because I'm very sincere when I say it. I will tell you

HOTEL GRUNEWALD
BAD NAUHEIM
TELEFON 2230

BAD NAUHEIM, DEN
TERRASSENSTRASSE 10

this much. I have never and never will again love any one like I love you sweetheart. Also I guarantee that when I marry it will be Miss "Little" Wood. There is a lot you have to understand though. Only God knows when the time will be right. So you have got to consider this and love me, trust me and keep yourself clean and wholesome because that is the one big thing that can determine our lives and happiness together. If you believe me and trust me you will wait for me and our future will be filled with happiness. With God's help it will work itself out and you will understand, and so patient I worked so hard to build up my career and everything and if you truly love me you would not want anything to happen to I and cause me to be unhappy. No matter what I'm doing, whether it be the army, making movies, traveling or singing I will be thinking of the time when we have our first little Elvis Presley. So keep this in mind and don't get discouraged and lonely. Just remember there is a guy that loves you with all his heart and wants to marry you. One more thing honey for goodness sake please don't let anyone read this and don't

HOTEL GRUNEWALD
BAD NAUHEIM
TELEFON 2230

BAD NAUHEIM, DEN
TERRASSENSTRASSE 10

say a word about this letter to anyone. you know
how I hate that so be careful baby. If you love
me and you are sincere you wouldn't want to
let anyone know our intimate secrets. I better
go for now love. so be happy and ~~rember~~ remember
down in your little heart that I love you,
love you, love you. keep writing

yours *alone and forever*

E. P.

P. S. I love you

(The second letter Elvis sent Anita from Germany).

My Dearest "Little" Darling,

I just received your letters and I can judge by the last 3 that you are a little disappointed. Well I can't blame you, especially since all that mess was written about "little puppy" and all that "horse shit". Well I don't know where they get the information but th[e] girl they speak of was a photographers model and she was brought over by some newsman the first week I was here. I have seen her one time since then. She doesn't speak a word of English and I have not been dating her and I did not say all that stuff about seeing her 4 or five times and I have not tried to keep anything from you. You see

(2)

that was really played up big because the papers figured it was good for German, American relationship. Do you understand? But don't you dare ever mention it to a soul because if you do I am finished in Germany. Just keep it inside of you and regardless of what you read or what obstacles come up in our way, please remember that I am yours my darling, yours, yours, yours, yours, yours. No one will ever take the place of my little in my life. Baby you will never know how lonesome and miserable I am. I will be so thankful to God when once again I am free,

(3)
free to return back to singing, making movies, and above all, returning to your little arms and lips. Every night I lay in my bunk, I see your little eyes and your little nose and it's almost like you are here, like you are pressed up close to me. I can feel your little hair on the side of my face and sometimes I get so excited and want you so bad I start sweating.

"Wow"

"Well so much for that"

Listen my love never doubt my love for you always trust me and believe me when I say that I love you.

"over"

It sure is going to be a blue Christmas this year. But in 15 short months it'll be over and as General MacArthur said, "I shall return". Have a merry Christmas darling and remember there is a lonely little boy 5000 miles away that is counting the hours till he returns to your arms.

If you get a chance try to locate a record called "Soldier Boy". Play it and think of me. By the way our song from now on is "Love me Forever" by Tommy Edwards. Every night I play it just for you.

P.S. No one now reads this OK!

Always loving and wanting you.

Yours alone darling
Elvis Presley

(The third and last letter Elvis sent Anita from Germany.)

35th Transportation Company
Light Truck
APO 757, New York, N. Y.

My Dearest Darling Little,

Well here I am. I'm out in the field for 30 days again and very miserable. There is only one consolation, and that is the fact that it's almost over, and I will come home to my career, friends, and most of all you my darling. Anita there are many things I can't tell you over the phone so I will try to tell you now. First of all I don't really know how you feel about me now because after all 2 years is a long time in a young girl's life. But I want you to know that in spite of our being apart I have developed a love for you that cannot be equaled or surpassed by anyone. My every thought is you my darling, every song I hear every sunset reminds me of the happy and wonderful times we've spent together. I tell you this because I want you to know my feelings

141

25th Transportation Company
Light Truck
APO 757, New York, N.Y.

toward you have not changed, but instead
has grown stronger than I ever thought
it could. I have hurt you sometimes because
I was mad at some of the things you did
or I thought you did, but everytime these
things happened I thought that maybe you
only liked me for what I am, and didn't
really love me for myself. These things
happen in life baby, misunderstandings,
heartbreak and loneliness, but the fact remains,
if it's really love anita, if we really love
each other it will last, and these things will
be something of the past, although things will
come up in the future that will hurt us
both. They are to be expected. I have had
feelings that in the last few months something
has happened as far as you're concerned, not
only because you haven't written but by
the sound of your voice when I talk to you.
The warmth and love seems to have dimmed,

142

have or would. Well we are all ___ the days untill we come home ___ I didn' I want you ___ on the ___ because in spite of the fact that I love my friends and relatives, when we first lay eyes on each other we will cling to each other like a vine. So I think some other people might I get their feelings hurt. So please understand honey. You have surprised me at how understanding you are. So darling if you still feel the same and if you love me and me alone we will have a great life together even though you hear things and read things and things as you said, "everyone knows how I feel about you." I can't explain to you how I crave you and desire your lips and your body ___ me darling. I can feel I now. the ___ need and the desire we had for each other a body"!! Remember darling, "True love holds it laurels through the age no matter how loud the clamor of denial." that which deserves to live ——— lives. yours alone

E. C.

Modeling for Holiday Inn *(from the collection of Anita Wood)*

Anita singing at the Black Orchid nightclub in Chicago
(from the collection of Anita Wood)

Out on the town, for publicity's sake, with comedian George DeWitt.
(Courtesy of The Harwyn Club)

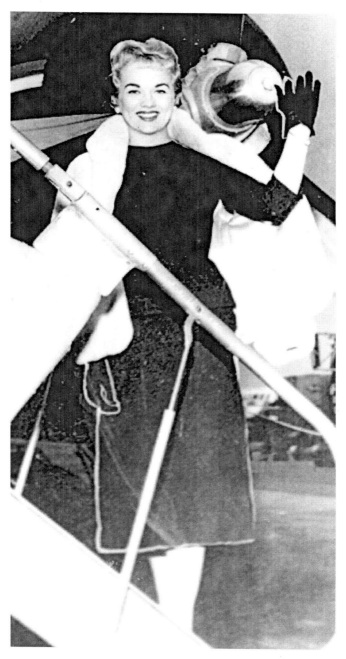

Leaving Memphis, headed to New Orleans. *(Courtesy of Memphis Press-Scimitar Morgue Files/Special Collections, University of Memphis Libraries)*

From the collection of Anita Wood

Anita's first single, with the flip side being "I'm Liking This."
(Courtesy of Dr. John Carpenter)

From the collection of Anita Wood

Envelope containing pictures sent to Anita from Elvis in Germany.

Post card from Elvis in Germany

This page, as well as opposite:
Front and back of photographs sent to Anita by Elvis

Anita working as a disc jockey at WHHM.
(Courtesy ofMemphis Press-Scimitar Morgue Files/Special Collections, University of Memphis Libraries)

Anita and Jimmy Arnn posing for an upcoming variety show, March 1959.
(Courtesy of Memphis Press-Scimitar Morgue Files/Special Collections, University of Memphis Libraries)

Top and bottom: Anita posing at the Plymouth dealership that gave her a convertible to drive, January 1960.
(Courtesy of Memphis Press-Scimitar Morgue Files/Special Collections, University of Memphis Libraries)

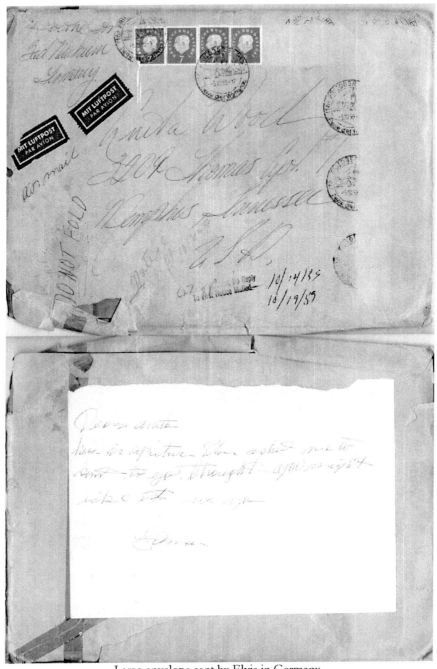

Large envelope sent by Elvis in Germany,
containing photos with note from Lamar

Elvis' Army photo
(from the collection of Anita Wood)

Alan Fortas and Elvis
(from the collection of Anita Wood)

Photograph of the guitar that Elvis gave Anita for Christmas
while he was in Germany. *(Courtesy of Heritage Auctions)*

ONCE UPON A TIME: ELVIS AND ANITA

Chapter 11

Sweet Reunion

On March 3, 1960, Momma went to Patsy Presley's house to await Elvis' arrival at Graceland. As you can imagine, the entire family was excited, and the air was filled with anticipation. Though Elvis knew that Momma was as eager to see him as anyone, he'd asked her to allow his family some time with him first, so that he wouldn't hurt anyone's feelings. It killed my mother to hear that, but in her heart she knew he was right. So she agreed to wait for his call — even when Patsy and her parents all insisted that she come along with them anyway, Momma insisted that she stay behind.

As it happened, she did not have to wait very long. About a half hour later, Patsy called. "Elvis keeps asking, 'Where's Little, where's Little?'" she said with glee. "You best high-tail it on out here." So Momma grabbed her purse, ran out to her car, and drove as fast as she could to Graceland.

Momma remembers the evening as being somewhat surreal. She entered Graceland through the back door, made her way through the kitchen and living room, and hugged various family members and friends, many of whom she hadn't seen in the two years since Elvis left. Then she saw him standing in the music room, his back to her. He was dressed in regular black clothes instead of his Army fatigues, which for some odd reason threw her a little. In fact, to this day my mother still cannot find the words to express exactly how she felt in that moment. But it was almost as if everything were frozen in time, and she could barely breathe.

Elvis must have sensed her presence, because right then he turned around and his eyes met hers. His hair had all grown out again, and once more he had dyed it black. He no longer had that golden tan from the Texas sun, and yet he looked just as handsome as ever.

His hands were on his hips. "Why, come here, Little!" he said with a smile and a wave.

Momma ran to him with outstretched arms, and he scooped her up and twirled her around. "I can't believe we're here!" he kept saying. "I love you, Little — I am so glad to see you! You look wonderful."

"I love you, too," Momma said. "I missed you so much and I'm so glad you're back."

They hugged and kissed and held each other for the longest time — in fact, Elvis hardly let go of her the entire night. Every time they'd mix and mingle with someone else, he'd lean over and kiss her cheek, forehead, or lips. Once again, everything felt right, as though they'd never been apart. Elvis was home, and so was she.

A little later on, Elvis sat down at the piano with Momma beside him and started playing and singing songs, including "Soldier Boy" and "Please Don't Stop Loving Me," both of which he sang just for her. They kept looking in each other's eyes before he finally said "Come on, Little," and took her upstairs to his bedroom. It seems he could not wait another minute to have her all by himself.

* * *

Elvis told Momma there wasn't much about Germany that he liked at all. "It was pretty to look at," he said, "but the people over there talked funny, and they all seemed a bit strange to me." He also talked about how cold he would get every night when he was out on maneuvers. (Being a singer, Elvis was always susceptible to throat ailments, anyway, but apparently he got even more sore throats than usual over there on account of the weather.) But he was happy to be back at Graceland, and grateful that his fans had been loyal to him while he was gone: "You won't believe the pile of mail that was waiting for me when I got home."

Above all, Elvis told my mother just how much he missed her. "How I wish you could've been there with me, Little," he said. "But it just didn't work out."

The more he talked, the more Momma could not keep her eyes off him. After all this time, he was really there, holding her and looking as handsome as always. It was wonderful.

One story that he shared that night was interesting, to say the least. Because Elvis had problems with acne when he was young, he was always looking for ways to improve his complexion. A dermatologist once told him that Neutrogena soap was the only kind of soap that he should use on his face and body. Elvis took the dermatologist's advice on skin care and had been using Neutrogena products ever since.

As it happened, Elvis met another dermatologist in Germany who had developed his own brand of face cream, and which he claimed would also improve Elvis' skin. Elvis agreed to try that one as well. He not only liked the results, but even brought home an extra jar of that particular face cream for Momma to use.

Now here's the interesting part. "I think that guy might be a little gay, Little, because he kept chasing me around the room," Elvis said. "I didn't have anything to do with him after that."

* * *

Soon life picked up almost if Elvis had never left. Momma continued to work, but came home to Graceland every night to be with him (and, when he was out of town, she'd sleep with Dodger, as before). One big change, however, was that, while in Germany, his father had met a woman named Dee Stanley. Elvis didn't like that at all.

According to Elvis, Dee came over to their house in Germany one night and tried to seduce him — but when he turned her down, she immediately latched on to his daddy. One night, after Vernon took her into his bedroom, Elvis looked through the keyhole. "I knew right then that he was a goner, Little. You wouldn't believe some of the things I saw her doing."

But Vernon was crazy about Dee, so out of respect for him, Elvis was polite to her. But deep down, he couldn't stand to see what was happening. "That woman is making a fool out of my daddy," he said. "She really knows how to work him."

Momma remembers the day when Vernon and Dee announced they were getting married. She was sitting next to him in the kitchen when they gave them the news. For a moment, she thought Elvis was going to fall out of his chair.

"Will you come to the wedding, son?" asked Vernon.

"No," said Elvis. He didn't say much more beyond that. Once they left the room, however, he could not stop ranting and raving about it to Momma.

One problem that Elvis had with Dee was he thought she was too aggressive — after all, she had gone after his father (Elvis, being old-school, believed that the man should pursue the woman). But the bigger issue was that he felt Vernon's relationship with Dee was too soon after his mother's death. Given how close Elvis was to Gladys, Momma completely understood.

"I do not approve of this marriage, Little," he said. "That woman is a liar and a man devourer. All she wants is whatever money she can get for her boys and for herself. There is *no way* in this world that I am going to that wedding."

And he didn't. Instead, he arranged for Momma and the rest of the gang to go swimming with him that day.

Elvis was not alone in his opposition to Dee Stanley. Dodger didn't care much for her, either ("That woman is a blonde-headed heifer," she used to say to Momma). Several other members of the family also despised her for taking advantage of Vernon when he was completely vulnerable.

As for my mother, she was nice to Dee, and Dee was nice to her. But knowing how Elvis felt about her, she kept Dee at an arm's distance. There was always something phony about her — to this day, Momma cannot see what Vernon saw in her, except that sometimes men are blind. After all, it had been a while since a woman had last doted on him like that, and perhaps he was just eating it up. Even so, apparently, while she was pursuing Elvis' father, Dee was cheating on her husband. Momma didn't like that about her, either.

165

That said, though Momma was not particularly fond of Dee, she did like both of her sons (Ricky, especially). At the very least, she felt sorry for them, knowing how hard it had to be for children that young to be removed from their father.

She remembers that whenever the boys saw Elvis, they'd always say, "That's my brother!" For his part, Elvis was always polite to them whenever they were present, but once they left he wanted nothing to do with them. "I am *not* their brother," he'd say with a shake of the head. Soon, however, Vernon had a large playroom built for the boys so that they could stay out of Elvis' hair, and that's where they spent most of their time. (Momma has since heard that Elvis became closer to Dee's boys in later years, and she hopes that was the case.)

Elvis tolerated the marriage, and though he hated it when Vernon moved Dee into his parents' bedroom, he bit his tongue. But when Dee started changing things around the house, that's where he drew the line. Eventually Vernon bought a house of his own for Dee and the boys near Graceland, which made Elvis very happy. Grandma then moved downstairs into his parents' old bedroom. That made Elvis happy, too: With Dodger getting older, he didn't want her to have to keep climbing the stairs every night to go to bed.

* * *

One development that Momma did not care about was Elvis' newfound fascination with karate, which he began practicing after taking some lessons in Memphis. When he wasn't driving her crazy with hitting and kicking stuff in the living room — or foyer, or anywhere else in the house, for that matter — he would grab Red and Sonny West, along with some of the other guys, to practice moves outside, while everyone else gathered in a circle to watch. Though no one was supposed to make contact, sometimes Elvis would slip in an actual kick or hit (while always making sure, of course, that no one ever hit him).

My mother has never liked contact sports (which is ironic, considering that she ended up marrying a professional football player!), so she simply looked the other way and hoped that this would just be a passing phase. But it wasn't. Elvis thought karate was the greatest thing, very masculine and powerful. Truth be told, though none of them would ever admit it, Momma thinks some of the guys were actually afraid to practice with Elvis, because they knew they might get hurt. But because they also worked for him, they couldn't afford to say no.

Fortunately for Momma, karate was not Elvis' only pastime. He still enjoyed renting out the movie theater, roller rink, or fairgrounds after hours. But he also liked to come up with new activities, often on a whim. One day, Elvis bought a bunch of remote-control airplanes, then drove out with the guys to a local school parking lot, where they could fly them. After a few successful takeoffs and landings, Elvis thought it would be fun if they all started crashing their planes into each other, with the winner being the plane that was still in the air. When that game was over, they just left the wrecked planes in the parking lot and continued driving around again until Elvis thought of something else that he wanted to do.

Elvis also liked to play touch football, which he and the guys did nearly every week. Then again, as with karate, whenever Elvis played "touch" football, you could count on real hitting and tackling. One day, Momma was on the sidelines watching him play when Elvis hurt his pinkie finger. Though he acted like it was no big deal ("Hey, look here, Little, my pinkie's crooked"), everyone insisted on stopping the game and taking him to the hospital.

Elvis seemed proud of his injury, as if it showed that he was really tough and could take it as well as dish it out. In any event, he insisted on driving himself to the hospital. Momma, as always, sat beside him. By the time the rest of the gang arrived, I would imagine that it had to be the largest gathering ever to accompany someone to the hospital with a broken pinkie!

After a while, someone from the hospital notified the press that Elvis had been injured. Before anyone knew it, photographers were lined up in the corridor, waiting to take pictures. Momma immediately put on her game face and looked away, as if she were not too concerned about Elvis (when, of course, she really was).

One day, Elvis found himself so bored, he went out and bought a new boat. Forget the fact that he was scared of the water and did not swim very well; it was just another one of those impulsive things that Elvis was known to do. As soon he got back to Graceland, he told everyone, "Get your swimsuits. We're going for a ride on McKellar Lake."

For a while that boat became Elvis' favorite toy. He'd ride that thing for hours at a time, and always very, very fast — which, of course, scared the dickens out of Momma. In fact, one time a press photographer snapped a picture of her screaming for dear life while she was water-skiing behind the boat. (Ironically, the purpose of the photograph was to illustrate how to water-ski safely with a life preserver.)

But that was Elvis. Sometimes he thought that he could get away with stuff that other people couldn't. In a way, he may have been right.

My mother once told me that having too much money is a bad thing, and never good. When I asked her why, she said, "If you have too much money, you can just go and get anything you want in this world — which gives you nothing to look forward to in this life. You don't have to work to save money for a house or a boat or a car or most anything else that you want."

Once he became a superstar, of course, Elvis never had to worry about money again. If he wanted something, he would buy it, and that was the end of that. But because he had everything at his fingertips, he had those moments where he could be bored and restless. That does not make for a very satisfying life, believe it or not.

* * *

Over the years various songwriters and record companies would send Elvis records or demos of songs that they had written for him, in the hopes that he might record them. Many times he would call Momma into his office so that they could listen to these recordings together.

Watching Elvis during these sessions always fascinated my mom. If he liked a song, he would listen for little things in the arrangement that he thought he could change or improve upon, so that he could sing it in a way that suited him. Most of all, he listened very intently to the lyrics; the lyrics needed to mean something to him before he could sing it. So long as the lyrics connected with Elvis, he could make the rest of the song work.

Some of the songs that came about from these listening sessions, he actually did record, including "My Wish Came True," "Wear My Ring Around Your Neck" (both of which Elvis thought were beautiful songs, though he did like the second one better), "Little Sister," "Don't," and "Marie's the Name of His Latest Flame."

Because Marie happens to be my mother's middle name, Elvis used to kid around with her about "Marie" ("This song is for you, Little," he'd say). They would always have a good laugh about that, but in truth my mom did not fit the part in that song at all.

* * *

In the meantime, the subject of Christianity would crop up from time to time, usually whenever someone that Elvis or Momma knew was hurt, had died, or had somehow hurt someone else. When it came to faith and God, Elvis could be moody: sometimes he was very willing to talk about it, while other times he'd change the subject.

Shortly after he came back from Germany, Momma told Elvis that she wanted to go to church on Easter Sunday. So he took her, along with some of the guys, to the Assembly of God Church in Memphis. They arrived a little after the service started, then quietly made their way into the balcony at the back of the sanctuary.

Elvis was hoping that they would go unnoticed, but when you're the King of Rock 'n' Roll, that isn't always possible. Once the congregation realized he was inside the church, all the worshippers started craning their necks, hoping to catch a glimpse. Before long, it reached the point where the members were paying more attention to him, instead of listening to the sermon.

"I'm sorry, Little," Elvis said. "But I think we should leave." They slipped out as quietly as possible.

Someone once said that being famous means the loss of anonymity. When one is as famous as Elvis Presley, it becomes difficult to do many of the things that you and I take for granted. That's why Elvis didn't go to church very often. Though he was spiritual in his own way, he also knew that he would become a distraction the minute he arrived.

Still, it bothered him that he couldn't even worship in a church, like anyone else. "Don't get me wrong, Little," Elvis said as they drove back to Graceland. "I love my fans, but they need to give me a little space."

* * *

For Momma's birthday that year, May 27, Elvis gave her a white gold diamond necklace in the shape of a bell, with a solitaire diamond hanging down from it. Two years later, in 1962, she had a portrait made of her wearing this necklace, along with a pastel pink dress and her hair up. It is a very becoming rendering of her, and the portrait hangs in her bedroom today.

Now when my mother originally had this portrait made, Elvis asked if he could have it and, of course, she gladly said yes. How it ended up back in her possession is a funny story.

One night when Momma was visiting her friend Jerry Gunn, Elvis invited some girl over for dinner. Unbeknownst to him, however, someone at the house gave Momma a call and told her what was happening. Momma told Jerry, and before long they were on their way to Graceland.

At the time Momma was driving Elvis' white Lincoln, a car that included a button that allowed him to open the front gate without having to wait for the guard. Knowing that, Momma pushed the button and drove right up to the house, without any advance warning.

"I want you to go inside and get my portrait," she said to Jerry. "I'll be waiting right here in the car."

As you might imagine, Elvis was dumbfounded when Jerry suddenly walked in and demanded Momma's portrait. But he gave it to her without any argument. Then, with the portrait in hand, and satisfied that Elvis knew he hadn't gotten away with this little stunt, Jerry and Momma drove off.

The next day, Elvis bought Momma another car of her own, a 1959 Montclair Mercury. He never once brought up the subject of the portrait.

Elvis bought Momma many other extravagant gifts over the years. One Christmas, he gave her a Lucian Pecard watch; on another occasion, he gave her a diamond and sapphire ring that was shaped completely different than the one that he had given her in Hollywood. (This ring, which my mother later gave to one of her bridesmaids when she got married, had two long sapphires with diamonds down the middle.)

Elvis also bought my mother nice clothes and other fine jewelry. But the most unusual gift of all was when he helped her get her teeth fixed. Momma once had a gap between her two front teeth, and she was always self-conscious about that. (When she hosted *Top 10 Dance Party*, the studio made her wear a mouthpiece that covered up that space.) Knowing that, Elvis arranged for her to see his dentist, Dr. Levine, about whether the gap could be fixed permanently. Dr. Levine said that he could cap her teeth, which would get rid of the gap and make them look better.

Momma had the procedure done and was very happy with the results. But what mattered most to her was that she paid for it herself.

In fact, as much as Elvis did for my mother, he never completely supported her. Knowing how much pride my mother had, he understood and respected that — except for a birthday or holiday gift, he never gave her any money. Now if they went out together, Elvis always paid for everything. But when it came to things like buying her own clothes, or going to the hair salon, or putting gasoline in her car, Momma took care of that herself.

* * *

Elvis could be very controlling, but in their five years together he never once told Momma how to dress, how to do her makeup, or anything else when it came to her appearance. No matter what she did, he always seemed pleased.

One time, for fun, she decided to dye her hair dark brown, just to see how Elvis would react. Sure enough, Elvis didn't recognize her at first: "Little, your hair is dark! What did you do to it? I can't get over it."

The more he touched it, though, the more he liked it. "That's okay," he said. "You're still my Little."

Years later, my daddy, Johnny Brewer, had a similar reaction one day after Momma dyed her hair from blonde to brown. By that time, he was playing for the Cleveland Browns, and he had been away all day at practice. When Daddy got home to the apartment where they lived at the time, he opened the door and did not recognize her. "Excuse me, ma'am," he said, "I must have the wrong apartment." He was about to turn around and leave when Momma burst out laughing.

Momma was a brunette for only a short time while she was with Elvis, but during that interval several pictures were taken of the two of them one night while they were at the fairgrounds. While on the Ferris wheel, Elvis said to Momma, "Act like you're scared, Little! Let's really make them think we're really scared!" So they hammed it up for the cameras, and the picture made all the papers.

Soon after those pictures were taken, however, Momma went back to being a blonde; after all, blondes do have more fun. Once again Elvis was caught by surprise, but he immediately liked it. "There's my Little," he said. "My little chicken head!" (Every time Momma changed the color of her hair, Elvis would affectionately call her "chicken head" because he thought that the smell of dye was like a baby chicken.)

In July 1961, Momma and Elvis attended the wedding of Pat, Elvis' secretary, and Red West. I've seen some pictures of that day, and neither Momma nor Elvis looked too happy. When I asked why, Momma said that everything was fine, except that when they arrived at the church, she and Elvis were mobbed by photographers. That upset Elvis very much, so my mom was just following his lead.

When she thinks about it, though, my mother wonders why Elvis acted so surprised. After all, his secretary was marrying one of his best friends; he should have known that the press, knowing that he would be attending the ceremony, would want to take his picture. (Once they got inside the church and away from reporters, Elvis calmed down, and he and Momma had a good time.)

* * *

Elvis' first Christmas at Graceland without his mother was a very somber occasion. Normally, he loved staying home for several weeks around the holidays, and always looked forward to spending time with his family and friends. But without Gladys around, he just didn't seem to care.

My mother did her best to comfort him. "I know that you are hurting, and I hate to see you this way. I miss your momma, too. But life has to go on, and you have to go on and do the best that you can. That's what she would want you to do."

Elvis did his best to put on a good front that year, but he never did get over the death of Gladys — and with Dee around, he could not stand to spend another Christmas at Graceland with her there. So the following year, 1961, Elvis spent Christmas in Las Vegas, while Momma stayed in Jackson with her family. On December 26, he sent her the following telegram:

DEAR ANITA WE TRIED TO CALL YOU XMAS EVE XMAS DAY AND TODAY I CAN'T GET THROUGH BECAUSE OF HEAVY TRAFFIC DUE TO THE HOLIDAYS I'LL TALK TO YOU AS SOON AS I CAN I HOPE YOU ALL HAD A NICE XMAS TELL EVERYBODY I SAID HELLO WITH LOVE E.P.

CTA896 OB422

O LGA649 PD FAX LAS VEGAS NEV 26 759P PST   1961 DEC 26 PM 11 09

MISS ANITA WOOD

   3764 HIGHWAY 51 SOUTH MFS

DEAR ANITA WE TRIED TO CALL YOU XMAS EVE XMAS DAY AND TODAY
I CANT GET THROUGH BECAUSE OF HEAVY TRAFFIC DUE TO THE HOLIDAYS
I'LL TALK TO YOU AS SOON AS I CAN I HOPE YOU ALL HAD A NICE
XMAS TELL EVERYBODY I SAID HELLO WITH LOVE
   E P.

Telegram from Elvis, sent on the day after Christmas in 1961
(From the collection of Anita Wood)

Chapter 12

Suspicious Minds

Elvis made seven movies in the two years after he returned from Germany in 1960: *G.I. Blues, Flaming Star, Wild in the Country, Blue Hawaii, Kid Galahad, Follow That Dream* and *Girls, Girls, Girls*. During this same period Momma released her second single, "I'll Wait Forever," with "I Can't Show How I Feel" on the B side. Both songs were written by Red Williams, and they talked about the relationship between Elvis and my mom.

Elvis particularly liked "I'll Wait Forever" — he thought the song was very pretty, and he loved the way Momma sang it. In my opinion, she and Elvis were being exploited, doing projects that so closely reflected what was happening in their lives, but that happens sometimes in show business. Nevertheless, they both remained very busy throughout this time, traveling back and forth from Graceland to Hollywood to Nashville to Las Vegas, and back again.

Momma accompanied Elvis to Hollywood while he was filming *Flaming Star*. This was the first time he invited her to be with him on the set, which Momma took to mean that he was getting closer to publicly acknowledging their relationship. (He would also arrange for her to join him on the set of several of his next few pictures.)

Barbara Eden (*I Dream of Jeannie*) and Dolores del Rio co-starred with Elvis in *Flaming Star*. An actress of Mexican descent, Dolores del Rio was one of the great divas of the silent film era (and, later, the Golden Age of Hollywood), but I understand that *Flaming Star* was her first movie role in nearly twenty years. Momma remembers that she would never smile off-camera, for fear that would give her more wrinkles!

Elvis wore really dark makeup in this picture, in which he played a cowboy who was also part-Indian. Since Elvis believed in life imitating art (at least, as far as whatever movie role he happened to be playing at the time), that meant that everything he did outside the production of *Flaming Star* had a cowboy-and-Indians theme.

When Elvis went off to do a scene, he'd tell Momma to go sit in his chair, which was canvas, just like a director's chair (except that it had his name on the back). Meanwhile, the rest of the guys would horse around in his trailer. It always struck Momma as funny how they always managed to have a ball, while Elvis was supposed to be working.

Just like he did in Memphis, Elvis loved to ride around Hollywood whenever he wasn't filming. While making *Flaming Star*, he had a white gold-speckled limousine with a sound system that people could hear, even if they were outside the car. Elvis thought that was great — he got such a kick out of driving around, knowing that the pedestrians and cars around him could also listen to whatever music he was playing. (Later, on another trip to Hollywood, he had a long Rolls-Royce that included a bar, and just about anything else you could imagine inside a car.)

One time, while driving back from California with Momma, Elvis was behind the wheel of a limousine, with a whole convoy of limousines behind him. At first he wanted to drive straight through to Memphis without stopping anywhere, but once they reached Las Vegas, Elvis changed his mind. They ended up spending several days there.

Elvis liked Vegas because it was a city that fit his lifestyle: he could sleep all day and still have plenty to do at night. Most of all, it was one of the few places he could go where he knew he wouldn't be mobbed. Now, mind you, when Elvis Presley sat down at the casino table to do a little gambling, people always recognized him, and some would ask for his autograph. But for the most part, the other patrons would leave him alone so that he could enjoy himself, just like anyone else.

As for Momma, this was her first trip to Sin City, and she had never seen anything like it. While the boys gambled, she would stay with Elvis, or sometimes eat at a nearby restaurant. Most nights, Elvis would take her to a show. One night, they went to see some elaborate production, where the women on stage descended one of those long staircases, while dressed in magnificent costumes. Momma marveled at the spectacle of it all... until she realized the women were topless! She was so embarrassed, she actually hid her face, while Elvis nearly died laughing. "It's just entertainment, Little," he said. "You don't have to look if it bothers you." Then he kept hugging her the rest of the night, which made her feel a lot better.

Once she got over her initial shock, my mother came to like Las Vegas and returned there several times. Once in a while, Louise, the wife of Elvis' cousin Gene Smith, would come along so that she would have some female company while the boys went off and played. Momma always liked Louise, and they became good friends with each other over the years.

Gene, Louise and their children lived close to Graceland. Sometimes, when Gene was away with Elvis on a long tour, Louise would invite my mom to stay at their house. One day, while Momma was staying with her, Louise thought it would be fun if she made up a press release for some future day after Momma and Elvis were married. This is what she came up with:

Mr. and Mrs. Elvis A. Presley and children — Elvis, Jr. and Lisa Marie — are announcing the arrival of their third child, Jeanie Louise, born yesterday at the Baptist Hospital. Both

mother, the former Anita Wood of Jackson, Tennessee, and baby are doing fine.
FLASH, FLASH, Oh Lord did you hear the child weighted 9 lbs and 11 oz?

Notice how Louise jokingly wanted Momma to name their third child after her. It was all in fun, of course, but what's really interesting is that my mother has kept that faux announcement among her mementos, even after all these years.

* * *

Momma also accompanied Elvis to Hollywood when he made *Wild in the Country*, which co-starred Tuesday Weld. Momma remembers Tuesday's long blonde hair, the gap between her teeth, and her two huge white German shepherds, which she kept on leashes. One day, Tuesday just showed up at the house where Elvis was staying in Bel Air, an exclusive community in West Los Angeles. She did not stay for very long, but she did walk around the kitchen and the billiards room with her dogs, while Elvis and the guys shot some pool.

Later that night, Elvis told Momma that "Tuesday is the craziest person you've ever seen in the world. She has a foul mouth, is as wild as anything, and is flat as a flitter."

"How would you know?" my mother asked. Surely, he had to have seen her with her clothes off to know what her breasts looked like.

Without skipping a beat, Elvis smiled and said, "Oh, you know what it's like here in Hollywood, Little. You hear stories."

Poor Momma. She loved Elvis so much, she was willing to believe anything he said. But that would change soon enough.

In the meantime, back in Memphis, Elvis was relaxing before production of his next movie when he received some shocking news: his cousin Junior (Gene's brother) was found dead in his home. Though not a regular member of the group, Junior hung around more often than he didn't, if you follow my drift. Handsome as a movie star, he was a crazy, lovable guy who liked to have a good time. But he drank too much and, unfortunately, that's probably what killed him.

Elvis, Momma and the others arrived at Junior's house before the police and ambulance. They found him on his bed, lying on his side; apparently he had just vomited in the moments before he died. It was a horrible sight to see, the kind of scene you think only happens in the movies. But it was real, and yet no one wanted to believe it. Even today, Momma still gets shivers just thinking about it.

Soon the authorities arrived and removed the body. A short while later, Elvis drove Momma and some of the others out to the funeral home where Junior's body was taken. There, a man led them to the area in the back where embalmment took place. Though each body was covered with a sheet, their feet, which by now were gray in color, were visible.

Being around so many corpses made Momma sick to her stomach. Yet Elvis found it all fascinating. He kept asking the mortician questions about the procedure: how the blood was drained from the bodies, and all the other preparations. Apparently there were some Jewish decedents in the room that day. "We will not drain those bodies," the mortician explained to Elvis, "because Jewish people do not wish to be embalmed." As gruesome as it was to her, Momma believes that Elvis' interest must have stemmed from the death of his mother just a few years before.

* * *

In the summer of 1961, while Momma was busy making appearances for AB-PT, Elvis went to Florida to film *Follow That Dream*, co-starring Anne Helm (*General Hospital*) and Arthur O'Connell. Vernon and Dee visited him on the set, while Grandma stayed behind at Graceland. When Momma returned home, she heard Dee go on and on about "how cute" Elvis and Anne Helm were. Dodger, however, assured my mom that she had nothing to worry about: "It's just talk, Neeter. Don't give it another thought. He'll be back home soon and in your arms, just like always."

Sure enough, Grandma was right; when Elvis came home, he told Momma that he loved her, and her alone, and that no one else mattered to him. That made her very happy.

Also that year, Momma returned to Graceland from one of her trips to find a chimpanzee in a cage in a room off the back hallway. Ever the prankster, Elvis told her that the chimp's name was Scatter and that she should shake his hand. Not knowing what she was walking into, as soon as Momma approached the chimp, he tried to pull her dress up! Naturally, Elvis thought that was funny, even after Momma screamed.

Meanwhile, a bunch of the guys were hanging out in the kitchen. When they learned what the commotion was about, they told Momma, "Consider yourself lucky, Anita. That chimp is the meanest thing you ever did see. He's already bitten some of our fingers!" Nevertheless, because Elvis found the chimp entertaining, so did the rest of the guys.

Later that year, Momma returned to Hollywood when Elvis filmed *Kid Galahad*, featuring Charles Bronson. Elvis played a prizefighter. He particularly enjoyed making this picture because, even though he had to sing a few songs, it gave him more of an opportunity to act than most of his other movies did. Plus he worked very hard on learning and practicing the various boxing moves that he had to perform on film.

Meanwhile, on the set, Momma was given the royal treatment. The makeup director, Lynn Reynolds, gave her a complete make-over, plus she gave her a beautiful shade of lipstick, which my mom liked very much.

One day, Elvis introduced Momma to Charles Bronson; the three of them sat and talked for a while in the back of the limousine. Momma thought Bronson was short and "rough looking" (meaning he had a manly face). He was very nice, and she enjoyed meeting him.

* * *

By now my mother understood that the one certainty about life with Elvis is that there would always be rumors about women, especially when he was on tour or off making a movie. While she never liked hearing these stories, by and large she knew to ignore them. Because no matter how many miles separated them, Elvis always called her — if not every day, then usually every two or three days — and assured her that she was the one.

One day she somehow came across one of those so-called "little black books." In it was listed the names of various girls from different cities across the country, along with their phone numbers. Momma was not sure whose book this was — the handwriting was not Elvis' — but it had to belong to one of the guys. Knowing that most of the boys in Elvis' entourage were either married or in a relationship, she did not believe this list was something he needed to keep (whoever "he" happened to be). So she tore those pages out of the book and put them in her purse.

Believe it or not, she still has a page of this list. And though I'm sure she may have wondered who these girls were, she never mentioned it to Elvis — or anyone else, for that matter.

One time, however, while Momma was staying with Louise, the press seemed to be circulating even more rumors than usual. As it happened, and for whatever reason, she had not heard from Elvis in ten days — even though Gene, who was with him on tour at the time, had called Louise several times during that same span. This made Momma believe that, maybe, just maybe, Elvis really was seeing someone "special" this time, and not just for publicity.

Knowing how livid this was making my mother, Louise said, "Anita, you have got to confront Elvis and tell him how you feel." She even encouraged her to go out on a date herself, just to make him jealous.

Though Momma hated the idea of confronting Elvis, she also knew that this was something she needed to get off her chest. So she picked up the phone and asked him why he hadn't called. As my husband would say, it was a fishing exploration, pure and simple. The conversation went something like this:

"I haven't heard from you in a while," Momma began. "You must be working real hard... or something."

"What ya talkin' about, Little? I talked to you about a week and a half ago."

"That's right, you did," my mother said. "But only because *I called you.* Seems that's the only time I do talk to you these days, is when I call!"

Elvis tried to smooth that over with a laugh, but Momma wouldn't have it.

"Well, you know I love you, Anita."

"I don't believe you do," Momma replied. "Don't you miss me?"

"Of course, I miss you," Elvis said. "You're my Little Itty-Bitty."

"Well, it sure don't seem like it."

"Well, it may not seem like it to you, Little, but that's the way it is. That's the way it is, and you know it." Then he tried to "baby talk" her, but Momma wouldn't go for that, either.

"Elvis, I am not a baby right now. I want you to explain why you haven't called me in a week and a half. You used to call me all the time when you were on the road — even if you had nothing to say, you always called at least twice a week. Tell me why I haven't heard from you, then maybe I will understand."

"There's nothing to explain, Anita. I think about you all the time... I just haven't thought about calling you. But don't worry, I'll be glad to see you when I get home."

"You haven't thought about calling me in a week and a half, and you tell me not to worry?"

"Aww, c'mon, Little, you know what I'm saying."

"No, I don't, Elvis. All I know is that you used to call me all the time when you were gone, and now I haven't heard from you. You don't know how big a difference that is."

"Ain't no difference, Little. You shouldn't feel that way about it."

"I can't help it, Elvis. When it comes to certain things, I'm just like any other girl."

"I know you are," said Elvis. "You're even sweeter than any other girl."

"Well, I'm not so sure about that."

"What do you mean by *that*, Little?"

She came right out and said it. "Do you have a girlfriend out there?"

"Do I have a *girlfriend* out here?"

"You heard what I said."

"Oh, don't be that way, honey. I've told you a thousand times, I'm crazy about you."

"Well, you're sure not acting like it."

"Anita, can't you take my word for it? If I didn't love you, I wouldn't be wasting my damn time with you. Just because I don't call you three or four times a week, don't mean that I don't love you. Don't go crazy on me now — every time I talk to you, you tear my damn head up!"

"That's not true, Elvis, and you know it!"

"Well, then, you ought to know by now how I feel after you, Little. I love you very much, I miss you very much, and if you were with me right now, I'd be perfectly happy!"

When she looks back on it now, my mother wishes that she had never made that call, because she and Elvis ended up arguing with each other for nearly half an hour. But at the same time, her gut kept telling her that something *was* different — that no matter what he said, he was not being faithful — and it was about time that she stop pretending to herself, and to everyone else, that he was.

Even so, their conversation gives us some insight into Elvis' feelings. I don't believe he was insincere that night when he told Momma that he loved her. But as my husband said when he first heard this story, no man would have put up with hearing her suspicions for half an hour unless they were actually true.

* * *

Meanwhile, Momma received some nice coverage in an article written by Albert Hand that appeared in the March 1962 issue of *Elvis Monthly*, a British magazine devoted to all things Elvis. Mr. Hand, who was also editor of *Elvis Monthly*, had flown out to Memphis a few weeks earlier to interview Momma at a family function held at Gene and Louise Smith's house. Elvis was out of town at the time, but Gary Pepper was at the party, along with his parents, Penny Fortune, and a Mr. and Mrs. Nichols. The article gives us a good idea of how Presley fans overseas perceived my mom's relationship with Elvis. Here's an excerpt:

> Another complex question in the British fan's mind over the years has been the question of Anita Wood. To the majority of the fans, she has always been a "mystery thing," and the articles that have seeped into this country from the states have rarely been very complimentary. However, due to the peculiar trait in the British race to always "root for the underdog," this fact alone has endeared her to the hearts of us here… a fact which we found a little difficult to convince our American friends during our visit. So we, on the eve of meeting her, were left in the middle of two general trains of thought: On the Stateside, in the main, branded as a "gold-digger," on the Britishside, "the girl next door."
>
> We found [Anita] to be an exquisitely dressed, smart young lady, blessed with looks, figure, friendliness, a heart that beats Elvis… vivacious, a brilliant conversationalist, had a delightful sense of

humor, and a heart that beats Elvis… A wonderful singing voice, an excellent disc jockey by reputation, bubbling with delight at seeing us… and a heart that beats Elvis.

I shall never forget that moment when, at the family party, after at least half an hour's pleading, we finally persuaded her to place her own recording of "I'll Wait Forever" on the turntable. And as the soft gentle voice echoed round the room to its conclusion, I saw Anita's face wet with tears.

The record reached its conclusion. There was a short silence. And a voice whispered softly to break the silence: "I guess that's the story of my life." It was Anita who had spoken.

We came away loving the girl who loved Elvis. As we asked our questions throughout our journey, we never really found the answer to whether Elvis will marry soon. A lot of people were firmly of the opinion that Elvis would never marry, because of the high standard he would set in comparing the right girl to his mother. Many people were of the opinion that Elvis would "play the field" for a long time to come. Some thought the Colonel would put his spoke in and crush all attempts, in view of the damage to his career. Some thought he would fall pretty soon… the first time he was caught off guard.

But among his closest friends, the odds were still on Anita getting her man. She is well-loved by the family, of that there is no doubt.

I hope her close friends are correct. Anita would make a good life companion for Elvis.

I've touched on many of the things that Mr. Hand wrote about in the fifth paragraph, including how important it was for Momma that Elvis knew that she loved him for who he was, not for what he had. (Indeed, as I noted earlier, that's precisely one of the reasons why Elvis so dearly loved her.) And as I ran across this letter while pouring through mementos for this book, I was moved by the sentiment Mr. Hand expressed about my mom in the article. She really was a Cinderella story, and it was touching to learn that so many fans throughout the world were pulling for her to win.

If only they knew that, within six months of the publication of this article, the fairy tale would come to an end.

When photographers showed up at the hospital after Elvis broke his pinkie,
Anita looked away and appeared to be disinterested, like she had been told to do.
(From the collection of Anita Wood)

Anita displaying the use of a life preserver while skiing behind Elvis' boat.
(Courtesy of Memphis Press-Scimitar)

Elvis gave Anita the diamond bell necklace that she is wearing in this portrait.

Anita's good friend Jerri Gunn, posing with her husband, Jerry Lee Lewis.
(*From the collection of Anita Wood*)

Make—No. Cylinders	Model No.	Model Name	Yr. Mod.	N.U.	Serial Number	Motor Number	Body Type	Use
Mercury 8		Mtcl	1959 Used			M9ZB 527060	4 Dr.	

Extra Equipment:	Transmission	Brakes	Steering	Radio	Heater	Air Cond.	Other
	Regular ☐ Automatic ☐	Mech. ☐ Power ☐	Mech. ☐ Power ☐	Yes ☐ No ☐	Yes ☐ No ☐	Yes ☐ No ☐	

If Truck, Truck Questionnaire Must Be Attached.

Car will be kept at No.................................(Street), ...(City), ...(County), ...(State).

Purchaser agrees not to remove Car permanently from the filing district in which said address is located without the written consent of Seller.

Purchaser understands that this contract evidences a transaction governed by the Tennessee law on Instalment Sales. By executing this contract Purchaser represents and warrants that he has been quoted both a time price and a lesser cash price and has elected to buy the car described herein for the higher time price and all negotiations leading up to the consummation of this transaction are merged into the terms and conditions of this contract which exclusively evidences his agreement and obligation, and further that he has received a true copy of this contract which was completely filled in prior to presentation to him and his execution hereof.

DESIGNATION OF INSURED

If the cost of any insurance, other than insurance on the Car, is included in the Total Time Price, Purchaser designates the individual whose signature first appears below as the person to be covered thereby.

☞ P. X................................(Seal)
(Purchaser Sign Here)

P................................(Seal)
(Purchaser Sign Here)

———— DEALER'S ASSIGNMENT ————

FOR VALUE RECEIVED, and pursuant to the Terms of Assignment shown on the reverse side hereof, Undersigned hereby sells, assigns and transfers to Commercial Credit Corporation, its successors and assigns, the above contract and all of Undersigned's right, title and interest in and to the Car referred to therein, with power to take legal proceedings in the name of Undersigned or itself.

Commercial Credit Corporation is hereby authorized to correct

FORM 1307 AF — TENNESSEE   ROF 5/61

patent errors in said contract and all other papers executed, endorsed or assigned in connection therewith.

Signed and sealed this 28th day of Feb. 19 62

Schilling Motors, Inc. ....(Seal)
(Dealer Sign Here)

................................(Seal)
(Owner, Officer or Firm Member)

ORIGINAL—FOR COMMERCIAL CREDIT CORPORATION

Signed contract for the second car that Elvis bought Anita.

A brunette Anita cuddles with Elvis at the fair.
(Courtesy of Brian Petersen)

"Act scared, Little! Make 'um think we're scared!"
(Courtesy of Brian Petersen)

(from the collection of Anita Wood)

More fun at the fair
(Courtesy of Brian Petersen)

Anita and Elvis at Red West's wedding
(From the collection of Claude Francisci)

Anita posing in front of Graceland with Vernon, Dee Stanley's sons and an unidentified relative or friend.
(Courtesy of www.elvismatters.com)

Anita guest-starring as "Miss Matzo Ball of 1960" in a local production.
(Photo by Ken Ross, courtesy of Memphis Press-Scimitar
Morgue Files/Special Collections, University of Memphis Libraries)

Elvis and Anita at the Fair in 1962
(from the collection of Russ Howe)

Elvis and Anita riding the bumper cars in Memphis.
(Courtesy of Brian Petersen)

Chapter 13

All Good Things Must Come to an End

One day in 1962, around the first of June, Momma was with Elvis in Hollywood while he was completing production of *Girls! Girls! Girls!,* co-starring Stella Stevens, which he made for Paramount Pictures. Though some of the film had been shot in location in Hawaii earlier that spring, Momma did not accompany Elvis on that particular trip. Now that he was back in California, she relished as always the opportunity to be with him on the road. But for some reason, she just did not feel like going out to the studio with him that day, so she decided to stay home and relax. She didn't realize it at the time, but that decision would change the course of her life.

At the time Elvis was staying at his home away from home in Bel Air. Among its amenities, the house had a huge library that was adjacent to Elvis' bedroom, and which was filled with books of all kinds. Always an avid reader, Momma decided to spend the day losing herself in the pages of a good book. She was going through the shelves, figuring out what she'd like to read, when suddenly she came across a book that was on top of Elvis' desk. She picked it up, flipped through the pages, and noticed there was a letter sticking out of it. The letter had already been opened; the return address was from Germany.

Curiosity getting the better of her, Momma took out the letter and read it. The letter was written by a fourteen-year-old child named Priscilla Beaulieu, the same girl that the papers had called "the girl he left behind" back in 1960, when Elvis returned from Germany. At the time, Elvis told my mother that Priscilla was simply the daughter of a friend who was an Army officer, and that she "happened to be a huge fan." That was it, end of story.

Well, to my mother's shock and surprise, as she continued to read that letter it became apparent that there was a lot more to the story than Elvis had led her to believe. Especially once she got to the part where Priscilla begged Elvis to let her see him in the United States.

Momma's mind was racing. If this were just another fan letter, it would be sitting in his office at Graceland. So why did Elvis have it with him? And why would any parent allow his teenage daughter to travel five thousand miles by herself to visit a twenty-seven-year-old man, even if he was a movie star and the King of Rock 'n' Roll?

The more she thought about it, the angrier she became... and the more it got her thinking.

It was very strange, even back in Momma's day, to be in a relationship with someone for five years and still not consummate it. While there is no doubt in my mother's mind that Elvis loved her, treated her with affection, and wanted her close to him, for whatever reason he did not want to take her virginity. Yes, they shared a bed together, and would rub up against each other at night, as young teenagers might do. Come to think of it, that's exactly how Elvis acted, like a young teenager — even though he was actually three years older than my mom. He liked it when they played together, such as when he had her bounce up and down on the edge of the bed, or show off her "granny" white panties. But their moments of intimacy never went past a certain point physically in their entire five years together.

They say that love is blind. When it came to my mother's love for Elvis, I'd have to say that's true. She always saw the good in him, and never dwelled on his negative qualities for any length of time. While they had their arguments, and moments of separation, they always kissed and made up. After five years, she liked to believe that she knew the real Elvis Presley, the man that others did not see — and in many respects, she did.

But as she looks back now, she realizes that there were things going on at the time that she either did not know, or did not want to know about — especially when it came to women.

Though she had heard all the gossip, and even knew that he was seeing other girls (dancers, starlets, wrestlers, singers, anything in a skirt), because Elvis always came home to her, she always managed to look past that. None of these girls mattered to him; only Momma was the one that he truly loved and eventually wanted to marry. He wanted a girl who was good and pure, and not easy, like the others. That's what Elvis always said to her, and that's what Momma believed.

But after five years, it was clear to Momma that Elvis was used to having his cake and eating it, too. This letter was the last straw.

* * *

Momma sat in the living room, stewing in her juices, until Elvis came home that evening. "Hey, Little, what's up?" he said, happy go lucky as always.

Though my mom was beyond angry, she would never make a scene in front of anybody. She quietly said, "Elvis, I need to talk with you for a minute. Can we go up to the library, please?"

Elvis looked at her kind of funny, but said, "Sure, Little. I'll be right there."

Momma walked upstairs to the bedroom and made her way into the library. Elvis followed shortly behind her. She opened the book, picked up the letter, and held it out for him to see. "Would you please tell me about this?"

198

Elvis' nostrils flared like a bull in the ring. "What are you doing looking at my letters?"

"This letter happens to be from a little girl named Priscilla Beaulieu," my mother said calmly. "I read about her in the paper when you were in Germany, and you assured me that she was just a fourteen-year-old fan who meant nothing to you. You told me that story time and again, but undoubtedly that is not true — she's coming out here to see you!"

Momma had barely finished speaking when Elvis went berserk. He grabbed her by both arms and shoved her across the hall, where she banged up against the folding doors to his closet. Then he picked her up, shook her several times and said, *"Why did you look at it, Little — why?!?? Why did you have to find that letter?!??"*

Momma had seen Elvis lose his temper before, but this was something else. For a moment she thought for sure that he was going to strike her.

Fortunately, however, reason prevailed, and before long Elvis calmed down. When he wasn't apologizing, he was sticking with his story that Priscilla "was just the daughter of an Army officer, nothing for you to worry about."

But by that point Momma had had enough. "I'm going to pack my bags," she said. "I want to go home tonight."

For a man who was accustomed to getting what he wanted, this was hard to take. My mother knew the truth about Elvis and Priscilla, and nothing he could do could change that.

Still, Elvis pleaded with her not to tell anyone about the letter, or of Priscilla's visit to Los Angeles. Though my mother was beyond upset at the moment, he knew that he could trust her — and she knew, deep down, that she would never do anything that could hurt him. She promised not to say a word until he returned to Memphis. Relieved, Elvis picked up the phone and made arrangements for her flight home.

* * *

The next morning, Momma had no sooner set foot in Graceland when the phone began to ring. It was the private line. Momma knew it could only be Elvis calling, but she didn't want to talk to him. And yet it kept on ringing.

Finally she relented and answered the phone. It was Elvis, all right. He asked about her flight, he made sure she was settled, and then he apologized again and again. "Please don't say a word about this," he said. "It would ruin me, if it got out. She really is just a child, and she means nothing to me. You are the only one I love, Little. You have got to believe me."

Momma kept the conversation short. At this point, she didn't know what to believe anymore, but again she promised not to tell anyone — and, other than confiding in Dodger, she didn't tell a soul. Eventually the entire incident blew over, or so my mother thought. But then, one morning in August 1962, it all came crashing down.

Momma was on her way down the back stairs leading into the kitchen for breakfast when she overheard Elvis speaking to his father. (A few of the guys may have also been present, but my mother does not remember.) From the hushed tones of their voices, it sounded very much like a heart-to-heart conversation. She thought about heading back upstairs when suddenly she heard something that stopped her in her tracks.

"Daddy, I am so confused, I don't know what to do," Elvis said. "I am having the hardest time trying to decide between the two of them. How do I choose?"

For just a moment it seemed like the whole world was spinning. But Momma knew exactly who he was talking about: Priscilla and her. Then anger and her Southern pride kicked in, and with a deep breath she marched down the stairs. No one was going to debate and struggle to choose between her and anybody else. Not even Elvis Presley.

By the time she reached the bottom step Elvis was completely surprised. She looked him squarely in the eyes and said, "I'm going to help you make up your mind about that because I'm leaving. It's done."

That was another first for Elvis. No woman had ever left him before; he had always left them. Desperately he tried to work his magic one more time. "Now, Little, you just calm down. Come on in the dining room, and we'll talk."

"No," said Momma. "There's nothing to talk about."

"Now, Little, you know you don't want to do this. Let's talk and we'll work this out."

"No," said Momma, shaking her head. "I've made up my mind. I'm through. You won't have to make that decision anymore. You can have her."

Elvis kept begging Momma to reconsider, but Vernon could see that her mind was made up. Knowing how much Gladys loved my mother, and believing himself that things would not work out between Elvis and Priscilla, he tried to impart some wisdom. "Ya know, Anita, sometimes if you separate like this, you'll get back together again."

"No," said Momma, fighting back the tears, "that will not happen because I am going to call my brother in Jackson and tell him I am moving away. I'm sorry it has to end like this, especially after all these years. But this is my decision to make, not yours, Elvis — and it is hard because I still love you. You were my first love, and it will be hard to get over you. *But I will do it.*"

By now Elvis, too, had tears in his eyes, and he listened intensely to everything she said. He knew that it would be hard at first for her to get an apartment on her own, since she had been living with him for so long. Not knowing what else to do, he reached in his pocket, pulled out a big wad of money, and tried to put it in her purse.

"Don't you dare," my mother said. "I don't want anything from you!" With that she went upstairs, called her brother Andy, and began packing her clothes and belongings. It was the hardest thing she had ever done in her life, because she knew she would not come back.

A short while later, Andy had arrived from Jackson, Tennessee and loaded Momma's things into his car. It was an emotional scene, and both Momma and Elvis were crying. Andy was upset as well, not only for his sister but also for himself; he'd spent a lot of time hanging out at Graceland, even when Momma wasn't there, and he thought for sure that she and Elvis would marry someday. When he had a moment, he shook Elvis' hand and nodded, but beyond that he didn't say a word.

Finally, once everything was packed, Momma turned to look at Elvis. "Oh, Little," he said, "I pray to God I'm doing the right thing by letting you go."

"You don't have a choice," my mother replied. "I'm going. Goodbye."

She kept a brave front as she and her brother made their way down the driveway and through the iron gate. Once they left the premises, however, Momma went to pieces. She had just left the one and only Elvis Presley; he was not only her first love, but her only love. They weren't apart for even five minutes, and already she was mourning his loss. How could she possibly love anyone else?

Then her thoughts turned to fear and despair. She had given Elvis the last five years of her life. While most of her friends her age were already married, she had put her life and career on hold for him — and now it was all for nothing.

All she wanted was to go home to her parents in Jackson, and soon that's she where was. Her mother and father were terribly sorry, but they completely supported her decision.

Not long after she arrived in Jackson, however, someone from the local paper had heard the news and gave my mother a call. Though still very hurt and angry at Elvis, her loyalty to him ran deep. When asked what happened, she simply said that Elvis wasn't ready to settle down, "and I don't know if he ever will." Then she spun the conversation in another direction by announcing the upcoming release of her next single, "Love's Not Worth It" (ironically enough), with the flip side being "Still."

* * *

At first Momma cried for three straight days — and though there were moments when she wanted to pick up the phone and call Elvis, she resisted every time. Yes, she loved him dearly, but she was not going back. She ended up staying with her parents for about three months.

Years later, my grandmother told me that Momma "about drove me crazy during that time. She kept following me all around the house, and didn't want to be left alone." Mamaw was worried, of course, because Momma took the breakup so hard — it really was like a death to her. Life as she knew it had suddenly changed, and she didn't know what to do. Eventually my mother saw a doctor, who prescribed tranquillizers for about a month. That helped her make it through.

Meanwhile, somehow through the grapevine Momma had heard that Elvis was very hard to live with during those first few days after she left (one of the guys, she recalls, said he was "a basket case"). Even so, knowing that didn't make her feel any better.

So what happened next? Well, after a while Jerry Gunn called and invited Momma to come to Collierville to spend a few days with her and her family, which my mother did. During that visit, Jerry said, "It's time to move on with your life, Anita. Come live with me in Memphis. We could get an apartment together, and I know someone who can help you get a job."

My mom thought about it and said, "You're right, Jerry. Let's do it."

At first Momma lived with Jerry's family, and soon she got a job at the Memphis courthouse with a man who held the position of Commissioner of Delinquent Taxes. Not long after that, however, she moved out of the Gunn family home to take a second job as a part-time, live-in babysitter to Mrs. Ann Reeves, a widow with four children. A fine Christian lady, Mrs. Reeves was about to marry a widower named Frank Duffy, who also happened to have four kids. It was a real-life *Brady Bunch* situation, and I suppose you could say that Momma was hired to play Alice.

These jobs were entirely new fields for her, and Momma enjoyed them both. But it wouldn't be long before the entertainment industry came knocking on her door again. Radio station WHHM asked her to sing on the air every Thursday morning (which she did), while various other organizations invited her to sing at their events (which she did as well). In the meantime, Red Williams continued to write songs for Momma about her life with Elvis, as well as find other songs that suited her vocal style. In the ensuing years she would release the following three singles: "Mama" (with "It Hurts Me to My Heart" on the flip side), "Two Young Fools In Love" (with "Memories of You" on the B side), and "Dream Baby" (with "This Has Happened Before").

Knowing that she never aspired to be famous, I asked my mom why she continued to make records. Her response was simple, and yet it made so much sense: She was a single, working young woman at the time. Making records meant extra money, and that helped her make ends meet.

Chapter 14

Close Encounters of the Elvis Kind

While working at WHHM, Momma got to know one of the station's owners, Harlon Hill, a former NFL All-Pro who played for the Chicago Bears. One day in 1963, Harlon told her about his friend Johnny Brewer, who at the time was playing for the Cleveland Browns. "Anita, I think you'd like him," he said.

Now at this point, my mom had gone on a few dates since ending things with Elvis, but none of them had captured her attention. Open to meeting someone new, she told Harlon yes.

"That's great," said Harlon. "I'll set up a dinner date."

"Oh, no," said Momma. "I have heard stories about football players; they can be kind of wild. The only way I'm going on a blind date is if you go with me — and it would have to be lunch, and then we would have to come right back to the station. If you don't go, Harlon, I'm not going." Harlon agreed to her terms and ended up taking them to the Catholic Club for lunch.

Now Johnny Brewer, as you may recall, knew exactly who Momma was. He was not only excited to have a chance to get to know her, but determined that she would notice him once and for all. Daddy was ruggedly handsome as a young man, big and strong and, as my mother would soon find out, about as different from Elvis Presley as he could possibly be. He was independent, liked his own company, and didn't need people around him all the time. He was not exactly a homebody, but he didn't need to be on the go all the time, if you know what I mean. He could not carry a tune in a bucket, but he appreciated good music. Though he was not overly affectionate, he let you know how he felt about you, and his feelings ran long and deep. And, perhaps most significant of all, he was not a boy in a man's body, but a man through and through. Momma said that in many ways, Daddy reminded her of John Wayne. Considering how much she admired Wayne, that was high praise.

Then again, Daddy was intimidated by Momma at first, though he tried not to let that show. As a matter of fact, after that first date chaperoned by Harlon Hill, Daddy went back to Cleveland and didn't call her for quite a while. (Momma was a little put off by that.) When he finally did call her, he asked her out to dinner (this time, by themselves), and my mom agreed. He took her to a nice restaurant in Memphis, and then they went to a nightclub that was owned by one of his friends.

This being their first "real" date, Momma expected Daddy to try to kiss her goodnight when he brought her home — all the other men she'd dated tried to kiss her on the first date, so why should he be any different? Her plan was to say "I'm sorry, but no," just as she'd done with all the others. Only thing is, Daddy didn't try that at all! Not only did that get her attention, it got her thinking, "Hmm, what's with this guy?!? Why doesn't he want to kiss me?"

Of course, I think that it's awfully cute, and more than a little ironic, that Daddy used the same tack on Momma that she had used on Elvis on their first date so many years before. But, as I say, it left an impression on her, and she wanted to see him again.

Before long, Daddy called Momma and asked her on another date. This time they went to the movies, and at the end of the evening, he kissed her goodnight. Being a good head taller than my mom, he had her stand on the front steps so that they'd be on the same level, which Momma thought was very charming. The more she saw him, the more she realized that she wanted to know him better.

Daddy was born on a house boat in Mississippi. His father was a commercial fisherman, and worked very hard for a living — a trait that Daddy inherited at a very young age, when he would help his dad with hauling heavy nets of fish into the boat every day. All that tough, physical work made my father extremely strong, which helped him excel in high school athletics. While he played every sport on an exceptional level, football gave him the chance to make a better life for himself when he was offered a full scholarship to Ole Miss. And although he suffered a debilitating knee injury in college that threatened his gridiron future, he bore down, fought his way back and proved the doctors wrong. He went on to become an All-American at Ole Miss (where he helped them win the National Championship), and an All-Pro in the NFL, where he played for ten seasons.

It wasn't long before Momma and Daddy developed strong feelings for each other. They saw each other whenever he could fly down from Cleveland, and always talked regularly on the phone. At one point, he even talked about getting an apartment in Memphis, but Momma discouraged that. "Don't get an apartment on my account, Johnny, because I will never set foot in it," she said.

Daddy agreed not to do that. But as it happens, it would only be a matter of time before he and my mom permanently got together.

* * *

Meanwhile, one day in late 1963, Momma was working at the courthouse when she heard a huge commotion in the hallway. She went out to see what was happening when, lo and behold, there was Elvis Presley and his entourage. Apparently he had some business to attend to that day at the mayor's office. It was the first time she'd seen him since they split up in August 1962, and for a moment her heart stopped beating.

As you might imagine, Elvis was as surprised to see Momma as she was to see him. As soon as he noticed her, he walked right up and pressed his arms on either side of her against the wall, so that she could not move.

Since she and Elvis both lived in Memphis, my mother always knew it was possible that they might run into each other someday. She just never expected him to act like this when that day finally arrived.

For a moment she felt weak in the knees and found it difficult to breathe. But soon she managed to collect herself. She looked up to him and said, "Hey."

To his credit, Elvis must have known that he had come on too strong, because the first thing he said was, "Little, are you okay?" Nevertheless, he continued to keep her pinned against the wall.

"I'm fine," said Momma.

"What are you doing up here?" he asked.

"I work up here," she replied.

"Hmmh," Elvis murmured. Then he looked down her body to her feet then back to her eyes and said, "Well, you sure do look good."

All she could manage to say was "Thank you."

Elvis realized he was acting nervously, and making Momma nervous as well. He smiled at her, moved his hands to release her, and said, "I guess I better go, Little."

"Take care of yourself," Momma said with a smile. Then she slipped on down the hall as gracefully, and as inconspicuously, as she could until she reached the restroom. Once she was alone, she realized that she was shaking. So she leaned against the wall, drew a deep breath and let out a huge sigh. "Well," she thought to herself, "At least now I know how I'd react the first time I saw Elvis."

Then she glanced at the mirror, fixed up her hair, and smiled. Right then, she knew that she was really getting over him, and that she could move on with her life.

* * *

Sometime later, Daddy and Momma were talking on the phone one night when he said, "You know, Anita, you have a really pretty first name, but your last name is hard to remember."

"What are you talking about, Johnny? It's Wood, W-O-O-D. How much easier can it be?!?"

"I'm just saying," Daddy said with a laugh, "I'm having difficulty remembering it. I think we should change it."

"What do you mean, 'change' it," Momma said. "Change it to what?"

"Change it to Brewer."

"Are you asking me to marry you?"

"I believe I am," Daddy said. They had a fairly short engagement and were married on June 13, 1964. They moved up to Cleveland during football season but lived in Jackson, Mississippi during the off season. Later that year, Daddy would help lead the Cleveland Browns to victory in the NFL Championship Game, which was the equivalent to the Super Bowl back then.

Two years later, in June 1966, I was born in Jackson, Mississippi. That was the year Daddy was named All-Pro with the NFL.

One year after that, my brother John Lee Brewer, Jr. was born in Cleveland. As it happens, 1967 was also the year that Elvis married Priscilla. "Well, he finally married her," my mother said when she read about it in the paper. If he had married anyone else, she would have been surprised.

The following year, 1968, Elvis' daughter was born. Momma was pleasantly surprised that he named her Lisa Marie. That, of course, was the name that Elvis and Momma would have named their daughter, had things worked out for them. She was amazed that he had still remembered that name, even after all these years.

* * *

One day in 1969, Daddy was at the International Hotel in Las Vegas on business when he invited the rest of our family to join him. By this time, he was playing for the New Orleans Saints; Daddy had requested that the Browns trade him there two years before, because of his increased business dealings down south in the New Orleans area.

As it happened, 1969 was also the year that Elvis started performing live in Vegas — and, wouldn't you know it, he happened to be appearing at the International Hotel. As a matter of fact, Momma had no sooner set foot in the lobby with my brother and me when she ran into a few members of Elvis' entourage. It had been years since she last saw them, and they all enjoyed reminiscing with each other.

At one point, one of the guys said, "You should come to the show tonight, Anita. Elvis would love to see you."

"I don't know," my mom hesitated. "I'll have to check with my husband."

"That's okay, bring him along, too. We'll leave two tickets in your name."

Sure enough, Momma talked to Daddy, and he said, "You go right ahead. Matter of fact, I saw the show myself last night and had a good time. You will, too."

So later that night, Momma put on a one-piece fitted black lace pant suit, then took her friend Eloise Goodwin to see Elvis perform. Once they arrived, one of the guys escorted them both to a table up front, right by the stage. As soon as Elvis took the stage, he walked right up to their table and said, "Hey, Little."

Momma said his show was really fantastic, and that he was as electric as ever. All throughout the concert, Elvis kept coming over to her table to sing parts of the songs to her. He made her feel very special that night, just like he'd done so many times before.

Just before the end of the show, Joe Esposito, one of Elvis' right-hand men, invited Momma to come backstage. "Elvis would like to say hi," he said.

"Is it all right if Eloise comes along?" asked Momma.

"Sure," said Joe. "The more, the merrier."

So Momma and Eloise followed Joe into this humungous room that was filled with people. Almost immediately my mother spotted the face of an old friend, Vernon Presley. "Why, hey, Mr. Presley, how are you?"

"Anita?" he said. "What a pleasant surprise. You look so good. How are you doing?"

They chatted with each other for just a bit, and then Elvis entered the room. He walked right up to Momma, gave her a big hug, and said, "Hey, Little, will you come with me just a minute?"

"Sure," said Momma. She followed him into a small private room off to the side. She was not surprised that he had asked to see her, and yet she was a little nervous. Though more than five years had passed since that day in the Memphis courthouse, she remembered as if it were yesterday how strangely he had acted. But something told her that it would be all right this time, and that put her right at ease.

The room had a bed and a chair. Momma took a seat on the bed. Elvis sat down right beside her and gave her another hug.

"Little, it is so good to see you," Elvis began. "How are you and your family?"

"I'm fine," said Momma. "We are all doing just fine. In fact, I just spent a few days with my parents in Jackson before I came out here."

"How many children do you have?" asked Elvis.

"Two," said Momma. "Jonnita and John. They are just precious and I'm very thankful for them."

"Where's your husband?" asked Elvis. "I've watched him on television playing football."

"He's here at the hotel," said Momma. "In fact, he saw your show last night."

Then Elvis flashed one of his boyish smiles. "If Priscilla knew you were here, she would be mad as the dickens," he said. "She would have a fit."

"Well, for goodness sakes, then, don't tell her!" she laughed.

Then Elvis patted my mom on the leg and put his arm around her. "Little, I want to ask you something," he said. "Do you think we made the right decision that night when you left? Do you think it could have been different?"

"Well, I'll tell you what, Elvis," Momma replied. "If it hadn't have happened that way, you wouldn't have your little Lisa Marie, and I wouldn't have my Jonnita and John — so I have to think that it all worked out for the best. That had to be what God planned for us, because we wouldn't have them otherwise."

Elvis looked at her for a few moments before he finally said, "I guess you're right."

They sat and talked there for a spell, while Elvis continued to pet her. She noticed that he seemed heavy-hearted, so she asked if he was happy.

Elvis didn't answer yes or no. Instead, he just said, "You make your own happiness."

Well, next thing they knew, an hour had gone by. "I should probably go," said Momma. "Johnny will be wondering where I am."

"Please stay a bit longer, Little," Elvis said. "It's been so good to see you and to talk about old times. Those years we shared together, they were the happiest in my life."

It touched my mother's heart to hear that, but she knew it was time to leave. She smiled, stood up from the bed, and said, "I should go."

"Well, it sure was good to see you, Little," Elvis said. "You look so good, and I really like that outfit — it looks so good on you."

"Why, thank you," she said as she gathered her purse. "It was good to see your dad again. Just like old times." Then she turned to him and said, "Well, I hope you will all be very happy, you and your wife and your little girl, Lisa."

That made Elvis smile. "Yeah, Lisa's a real doll."

"I'm sure she is," Momma said. "I've seen pictures of her. She looks just like you!"

Elvis stood up and walked her to the door. "It's been great to see you again, Little. I can't tell you how much I've missed you."

"It was good to see you again," Momma said. "And thank you for letting me see the show. I really enjoyed it."

With that, he gave her one last hug and let her out the door.

"Well, imagine that," Momma thought to herself as she made her way back to Eloise. "He has a wife and a child, and yet he wonders if it was a mistake that we broke apart. He still wonders what life might have been like if we had stayed together." Still, it gave her some satisfaction that he even thought about her at all.

Then she realized that, even after all this time, they were still connected on a special level. No matter what happened in their individual lives, that would never change.

* * *

In 1970, Daddy retired from professional football after ten seasons. In his NFL career he not only never missed a regular season game due to an injury, but started at three different positions: linebacker, tight end, and defensive end. That was not unusual when my father played, but it's highly unheard of today. His coaches always told him that it could take as long as three months to learn a new position. Whenever he heard that, Daddy would just shake his head and say, "Just give me two weeks" — and that was all it took. He was one tough man.

When we left New Orleans, we moved to the Mississippi Gulf Coast, where Daddy had business in the real estate and insurance industries. That's also where Momma and Daddy had another son, Bradley Sean Brewer. When my brothers and I were young, we moved again to my dad's hometown of Vicksburg, Mississippi, where we attended Redwood Elementary School, the same school where he had graduated. Though we've moved around a bit over the years, our family has more or less lived in Mississippi ever since.

August 1973 was a very bad month for my family. Momma's father, W.A. Wood, had a massive heart attack at the age of fifty-seven. Momma flew to Memphis, and one of her brothers drove her to the hospital in Jackson where her father had been taken. He died shortly after she arrived. That was quite a shock, especially for my mom. He was always a rock in her life, the one to whom she could always turn whenever she felt troubled; his death, especially as sudden as it was, completely devastated her. Daddy drove up to Jackson for the funeral then returned home, while Momma stayed in town for about a month to help her mother.

While in Tennessee, Momma visited her friend Jerry Gunn, who by this time was married to Jerry Lee Lewis. As it happened, it was also around this time that Momma heard the news that Elvis and Priscilla had been divorced. That also came as a shock. (August had proven to be a sad month for Elvis as well. That was also the month when Gladys Presley died in 1958.)

While talking to Jerry, Momma got to thinking about the time when Elvis lost his mom. Back then, she could never fully understand what he had been going through — but now all of a sudden she did.

"You should give him a call, Anita," Jerry said. "Elvis would appreciate that."

"Oh, I'd love to do that," Momma replied. "But I wouldn't know how to reach him."

"I'll take care of that," Jerry said. And she did.

Elvis was still performing in Vegas when Jerry got him on the phone. Momma will never forget that conversation — it was the first time she talked to him since the time of their breakup in which he did not sound like himself. His words were slurring together (Momma believes he was on medication), and he talked very slowly.

"Elvis, I want to tell you something," she began. "You remember when your momma passed away, how upset you were, and how I had a little trouble understanding?"

"Yeah, Little, I remember," Elvis replied. "Why do you ask?"

"Because I want you to know that my father just passed away very suddenly, and now I know exactly why you were so bereaved," she continued. "You were hurting back then, and I felt bad that I could not share your pain — but now I understand. I wanted to let you know that. You know that I loved your mother, and I hated to see her die — but I didn't understand to what extent your feelings were, until my dad died."

Suddenly Elvis' voice picked up, as if he had regained his purpose. "This is what I want you to do, Little. I want you to sit down in a relaxed position with your spine erect. Close your eyes and inhale, now exhale." Momma did just that.

Then Elvis said, "Now, breathe normally, Little, and say to your inner self, 'Calm down.' Then get a pencil and paper write this down, word for word:

> Why is it one cannot quite realize,
> What a blessing true love can be?
> Must one lose love to know it is priceless?
> Must one be blind before one can see?
>
> Where does love go when it leaves us,
> The question will always remain
> For we can never know the answer
> Until we find love once again.

"Did you get all that, Little?" Elvis asked when he finished reciting.

"Yes, I did," said Momma.

"That's good," said Elvis. "Now read it back to me," which she did.

Then he said, "I want you to read that from time to time and think about what it says. Remember it. Read it whenever you feel lonely. I know it will bring you some peace."

"Thank you, Elvis, I appreciate this so much," my mother said. "And please forgive me for not fully understanding back then."

"Don't give it another thought, Little," Elvis said. "And I am sorry about your dad."

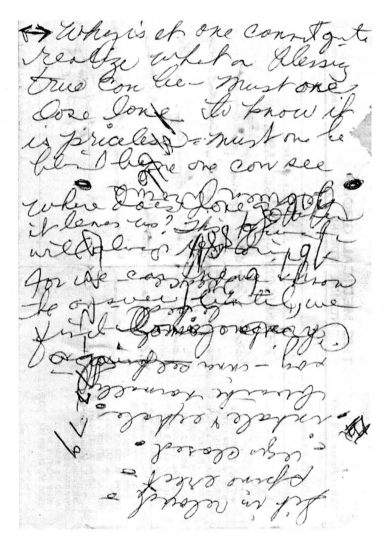

Actual scrap of paper on which Momma wrote down the poem that Elvis recited to her in August 1973, when she told him about the death of her father. As you can see, she started writing the poem on the other end of the paper.

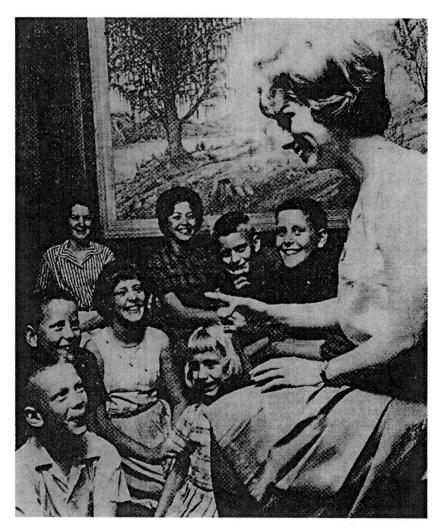

Anita in her new role as part-time live-in babysitter to the eight children in the blended families of Ann Reeves and Frank Duffy. *(Courtesy of Memphis Press-Scimitar)*

Photos courtesy of Dr. John Carpenter

Photos courtesy of Dr. John Carpenter

Photos courtesy of Dr. John Carpenter

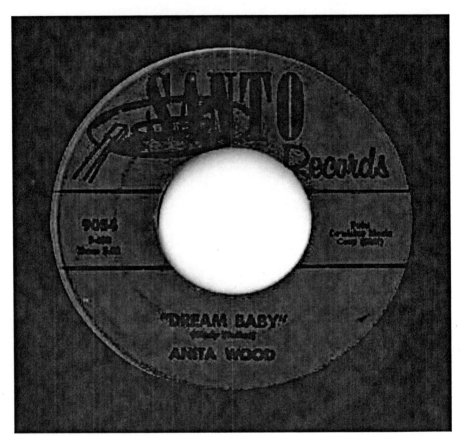

Photos courtesy of Dr. John Carpenter

In recording studio, December 1963. *(Courtesy of Memphis Press-Scimitar Morgue Files/Special Collections, University of Memphis Libraries)*

From the collection of Anita Wood

From the collection of Anita Wood

Anita sang every Thursday morning on *Good Morning From Memphis*.
(Courtesy of Memphis Press-Scimitar Morgue Files/Special Collections, University of Memphis Libraries)

Football trading card of Johnny Brewer

Johnny and Anita relaxing on a date

Johnny at a Cleveland Browns football practice.

Johnny and Anita with Gary Pepper on their wedding day, June 13, 1964.
Gary is wearing the ring that Elvis gave Anita right before he left for Germany
(*see insert*), which she wore on a chain around her neck.

Johnny and Anita with Cleveland Browns quarterback Jim Ninowski and his wife at a Jim Brown movie premiere. The jacket Anita is wearing was given to her by Elvis (Anita had told Johnny that she didn't have anything nice to wear that night). The next Christmas, Johnny bought her a mink.

Family picture taken shortly before Elvis died.
Clockwise from Johnny: Anita, Jonnita, John, Sean

Chapter 15

Final Goodbye

Life went on and, like many families, our family had some tough times, but somehow we made it through. My parents were always there for us as children, and still are today.

Though both Momma and Daddy were celebrities in their own right, they never forgot where they came from, and never once encouraged us to seek the spotlight. Instead they raised us with the same values that their parents had instilled in them so many years before.

Still, because my mother and father were both famous, there were moments growing up when I was afraid that I would never measure up to them. Whenever that happened, Momma especially would remind me that, for all its trappings, the life of a celebrity is not always what it seems. Above all else, she and Daddy wanted us to be happy... and from what they knew of fame, it didn't usually result in a happy ending.

In 1972, the *Commercial Appeal*, the local paper in Memphis, published an article stating that my mom had divorced my dad and furthermore, that she had gone to Las Vegas for a "reunion" with Elvis in his hotel room. Everything about this story was false and, as you can imagine, Daddy was not happy at all with what it implied. They sued the paper and won, but because the *Commercial Appeal* had deep pockets, it appealed the ruling three times. Though Momma and Daddy won each time in court, they never saw a dime of the money. (My parents remained married until Daddy died in May 2011, one month shy of what would have been their forty-seventh wedding anniversary.)

Sometimes I wonder what Elvis thought of that report in the *Commercial Appeal*, assuming he was even aware of it. Then again, he was so accustomed to publications reporting wrong information about him, I doubt he would have given it a second thought.

* * *

As I say, August has always been a sad month in our family's life. August 1977 proved to be no different.

Momma was blue to begin with when she woke up on the morning of Tuesday, August 16. It was the day before the four-year anniversary of the death of her father, so he was very much on her mind.

At some point that day our phone rang. Being eleven years old at the time, I raced to answer it. As it happened, it was my friend from school, Donna

Roberts, but she was calling about my mom. "How is she taking the news?" she asked.

"What news?" I said. We had not watched any television that day, nor listened to the radio. In fact, I believed we had all been out in the yard most of the day.

"I just heard on the radio that Elvis just died," said Donna. "I'm sorry, but I thought you knew."

Immediately I turned and looked at my momma; she was standing there right beside me. I knew that Elvis was her first love. She had told me all of the stories of their life together, and I could tell that, in some ways, she still loved him, even after all these years. And yet I didn't know what to say.

"What's wrong, Jonnita?" Momma asked.

"Momma, Elvis is dead," I said.

At first my mother looked puzzled, as if this couldn't possibly be true. "There must be a mistake," she said. "They must be talking about Mr. Presley, Elvis' father."

I was about to call my friend back and ask, when the phone rang again. This time it was a newspaper reporter, asking for a statement from Momma about the death of Elvis Presley. At that point, she knew the news was true, and yet she still refused to believe it. Elvis was too young, with so much yet to offer. It was hard for her to imagine a world without him in it.

She did not answer the phone that day, nor for several days after. She spent much of that time in her room, grieving in silence, though there were moments when I could hear her crying. But as upset as she was, she always pulled herself together by the time Daddy got home.

* * *

The funeral was held at Graceland two days later, on Thursday, August 18, 1977. As much as Momma wanted to be there, and as badly as she wanted to see Vernon and Dodger, she knew that the house would be swarming with reporters and she wanted no part of that at all. So she waited for a few months before heading up to pay her respects.

That brings us to that day where this story all began, when Momma, Mamaw, Aunt Karen and me went to Graceland in late December 1977.

When it was time to leave, Vernon, Dodger and Priscilla invited Momma to visit Elvis' gravesite. "Thank you kindly, but no," she said. "I know that he is up in Heaven, and I don't wish to see where his body is laid to rest."

Truth be told, Momma knew that, had she gone to see Elvis' gravesite, she would have completely fallen apart. That was not a side of her that she wanted Priscilla to see.

After Momma kissed and hugged Dodger one last time, Priscilla walked us out to the car. "Well, I'm glad I got to meet you, Anita," she said. "Elvis talked so much about you."

"I'm glad to have met you, too," Momma replied. "You have been very nice."

"You're welcome to come back anytime," Priscilla said. And with that, we waved our final goodbyes and left.

As we drove away from Graceland, my mother turned and looked out the back window. From the back seat, I watched her closely and noticed tears welling in her eyes. So many happy moments of her life took place inside the walls of Graceland - wonderful, intimate, fun-filled memories that all came back in a rush as the tears began rolling down her face.

She thought back to that day in 1962 when she and Elvis parted ways. So much had changed in her life since then, but she always held a part of him in her heart, and felt that he had a part of her in his heart as well.

Graceland had practically been home to Momma during her five years with Elvis, and leaving it had never been easy. But this was different, like one of those moments in life where the truth suddenly hits us, and we are overwhelmed. I could see the realization in my momma's face that the fairy tale was truly over... the King was dead.

Bibliography

Most of the information in this book is based on the recollections of my mother, Anita Wood Brewer, and my grandmother, Dorothy Wood.

The following resources were also extremely helpful:

Books

Guralnick, Peter and Jorgensen, Ernst, *Elvis Day by Day*. New York: Ballantine Books, 1999.
Guralnick, Peter, *Careless Love The Unmaking of Elvis Presley*. New York: Back Bay Books, 1999.
~ *Last Train To Memphis The Rise of Elvis Presley*. New York: Back Bay Books, 1994.

Articles

"6 Out of 69 — Reaching for Film Fame," *Memphis Press-Scimitar*, August 14, 1957.
"9 Hopefuls Await Magic Touch," *New Orleans States*, August 30, 1957.
"A Diamond and Eighteen Sapphires to Anita From Elvis," *Memphis Press-Scimitar*, 1957.
"A Goodby Kiss," *Memphis Press-Scimitar*, March 1958.
"Alexander Cheer Leaders," *The Jackson Sun*, October 30, 1949.
Alexander, J. T., "Visiting Anita Wood, Starlet, 'Loves' Knox," *Knoxville News Sentinel*, April 4, 1959.
"Anita and Friend," *The Light San Antonio Texas*, May 22, 1958.
"Anita and That Ring," *Memphis Press-Scimitar*, September 1957.
"Anita Straightens Out BB On Her Opinion of Elvis," *The New York Post*, September, 1958.
"Anita Tells Elvis: Visit Tops Letters," *The Commercial Appeal*, 1958.
"Anita Tells Her Own Story In 'TV and Movie Screen,'" *The Jackson Sun*, August 24, 1958.
"Anita Wood," *Memphis Press-Scimitar*, September 18, 1958.
"Anita Wood," *Memphis Press-Scimitar*, September 30, 1959.
"Anita Wood Appears in Short-Subject," *The Jackson Sun*, 1957.
"Anita Wood Named Signal Co. Sponsor," *The Jackson Sun*, 1954.
"Anita Wood Sings Friday," *The Commercial Appeal*, September 26, 1958.
"Anita Wood Winner of Talent Contest," *The Jackson Sun*, 1954.
"Bailey, Miss Wood, Win D.A.R. Medals In 50th Competition," *The Jackson Sun*, May 2, 1956.

"Big Adventure," *Memphis Press-Scimitar*, December 14, 1954.

"Blond Bait," *Memphis Press-Scimitar*, July 10, 1957.

Bruning, Bill, "For the Record," *The Commercial Appeal*, 1960.

~ "Variety Humming; Anita Is A Hit," *The Commercial Appeal*, February 16, 1961.

Burk, Bill, "Anita Flies Into Arms of Elvis," *Memphis Press-Scimitar*, September 14, 1957

Burrous, Georgia, "'Pince Me,' Says Anita Memphis Belle Wins Star Hunt," *New Orleans States*, August 31, 1957.

"Bye-Bye Memphis!" *Memphis Press-Scimitar*, November 6, 1957.

"Carnival Theme is Emphasized at the Sub Deb Summer Dance," *The Jackson Sun*, 1952.

"Cast of 'Trippin' Around' To Rehearse Monday Night," *The Jackson Sun*, October 11, 1953.

"CBC Homecoming Queen," *The Commercial Appeal*, 1958.

"Chance of Fame for Mid-South Youth," *Memphis Press-Scimitar*, July 9, 1957.

"Charm of Cricket On The Hearth Hold Firstnighters Spellbound," *The Jackson Sun*, 1952.

"Contest Won by Anita Woods," *The Times-Picayune*, August 31, 1957.

Dale, Marian, "Elvis' No. ? Girl On Her Own," *Fort Lauderdale News*, March 27, 1959.

"Elvis and Party See His Film," *Memphis Press-Scimitar*, June 1958.

"Elvis Coming Home: Things Will Soon Look Lively Around Here," *Memphis Press-Scimitar*, March 3, 1960.

"Elvis' Friend," *New Orleans States*, August 30, 1957.

"Elvis' Parents Think His New Film Is 'Terrific'," *Memphis Press-Scimitar*, July 10, 1957.

"Elvis Rumored Engaged To Honey Blonde Starlet," *The Jackson Sun*, 1958.

"Elvis 'Sweet' Says Beaut Laying Claim to 'Steady'," *New Orleans States*, August 31, 1957.

"Elvis to Anita: Diamond, 18 Sapphires," *Memphis Press-Scimitar*, September 1957.

"Emergency Visit," *The Commercial Appeal*, August 13, 1958.

"Everything From Jazz to Magic In 'A Little Bit Of Everything,'" *The Jackson Sun*, May 28, 1954.

"Fashion Extravaganza Guest Stars," *Memphis Press-Scimitar*, June 18, 1959.

Gaither, Ruby, "Blond Anita Soon to Sing For a Chance at Bigtime," *Memphis Press-Scimitar*, July 18, 1955.

"GI and the Girl He Left Behind," *New York Journal-American*, September 20, 1958.

"Guard Presents Second Act Of 'Pass In Review,'" *The Jackson Sun*, April 28, 1955.

Hand, Albert, "Move a little closer... to Elvis," *Elvis Monthly magazine*, March 1962.

Hochuli, Paul, "Elvis' Favorite Gal Had Rather Sing Ballads Than Rock 'n' Roll," *The Houston Press*, 1957.

"Home for Christmas," *The Commercial Appeal*, December 18, 1958.

Howard, Edwin, "2 Winners in Mid-South Hunt!" *Memphis Press-Scimitar*, August 23, 1957.

~ "About That Big 'Break' They Gave Anita Wood," *Memphis Press-Scimitar*, 1958.

~ "Anita Ends Her New Orleans Engagement," *Memphis Press Scimitar*, January 31, 1959.

~ "Anita Is Trying for Role In Play by Williams," *Memphis Press Scimitar*, 1959.

~ "Anita Ready for Work After Big Week End," *Memphis Press-Scimitar*, September 9, 1957.

~ "Anita Wood May Return to Memphis Tomorrow," *Memphis Press-Scimitar*, September 12, 1957.

~ "Anita's Singing Is Big Hit On Paar Show," *Memphis Press-Scimitar*, October 1958.

~ "Engaged? No, Says Anita — 'Just a Gift'," *Memphis Press-Scimitar*, September 1957.

~ "Exclusive News About a Pair Of Pretty Memphis Blonds," *Memphis Press-Scimitar*, 1958.

~ "'Hi, Honey!' – Elvis and Anita Keep in Touch Via Transatlantic Phone," *Memphis Press-Scimitar*, October 7, 1958.

~ "'I Told You So, Baby,' Elvis Says to Anita," *Memphis Press-Scimitar*, August 31, 1957.

~ "Lightning Hits Anita Again!" *Memphis Press-Scimitar*, September 7, 1957.

~ "Seven Beauties Talking — The Topic: Hollywood," *Memphis Press-Scimitar*, 1957.

~ "She Will Get Part in Film and a 7-Year Contract," *Memphis Press-Scimitar*, August 31, 1957.

~ "Stars of Today and Tomorrow Will Shine," *Memphis Press-Scimitar*, August 20, 1959.

~ "The Matzo Ball Game Looks Like a Big Hit," *Memphis Press-Scimitar*, March 18, 1960.

~ "Tomorrow Night, You Can Sit in on the Birth of a Star," *Memphis Press-Scimitar*, July, 30, 1958.

"In Grief," *The Commercial Appeal*, August 15, 1958.

"Is Anita Wood Getting A Real Break in TV?" *Memphis Press-Scimitar*, 1958.

"Jackson's Anita Youngest Disk Jockeyette?" *The Jackson Sun*, 1955.

"Jaycees Set Feb. 25 as Date for Music Show Here; Anita Wood, Bill Black Share Billing," *The Daily Dunklin Democrat*, February 8, 1960.

Johnson, Robert, "Anita Wood on Paar Show," *Memphis Press-Scimitar*, June 4, 1958.

Johnson, Robert, "Anita Wood to Replace Susie as Wink's Partner," *Memphis Press-Scimitar*, May 24, 1957.

~ "Jack Paar Tries to Explain Elsa's Blast at Our Anita," *Memphis Press-Scimitar*, 1958.

~ "Phone Call From Elvis: 'Home March 3,'" *Memphis Press-Scimitar*, October 15, 1959.

~ "Tonight: A Memphis Mystery (?) Guest," *Memphis Press-Scimitar*, July 3, 1958.

"Just Looking," *Memphis Press-Scimitar*, March 18, 1958.

Kahn, Dave, "Elvis' Girl Visits on LI: She Doesn't Miss Him!" *Newsday*, 1958.

Kleiner, Dick, "Anita Wood Sings For Andy Tonight," *New York World Telegram and Sun*, August 14, 1958.

Long, James, "Anita Home In Elvis' New Imperial," *The Jackson Sun*, October 3, 1957.

~ "Anita Signed by Hollywood," *The Jackson Sun*, September 1, 1957.

~ "Anita Wood Crowned Miss Madison County," *The Jackson Sun*, June 10, 1956.

"Marching Together: Elvis and Anita," Memphis Press-Scimitar, 1958.

Meanley, Tom, "Launch Fair's Sternwheeler With Unexpected Ducking," *Memphis Press-Scimitar*, September 1957.

Means, John, "Jackson Teen-Agers Join Famous Troupe For 'Sabrina Fair,'" *The Jackson Sun*, February 5, 1956.

~ "'Miss Tennessee' Madison, Jackson Are Runners-Up In State Pageant," *The Jackson Sun*, July 29, 1956.

~ "Local Entrants Await Pageant Competitors," *The Jackson Sun*, 1956.

"Mid-South Fair Talent Contests Start Many on Success Road," *Memphis Press-Scimitar*, August 11, 1955.

"Miss Anita Wood On TV Wednesday," *The Jackson Sun*, 1951.

"'Miss Madison' To Be Hostess Of The Fair," *The Jackson Sun*, September 1956.

Mitchell, Henry, "Anita Wood To Take Over As WHHM's Disk Jockey," *The Commercial Appeal*, August 27, 1959.

~ "Elsa's Barrage of Words Verval Beating For Anita," *The Commercial Appeal*, October 27, 1958.

"Movie Career for Anita?" *The Jackson Sun*, August 23, 1957.

"Movie Stars Arrive Here Tonight at 7," *The Austin American*, November 11, 1957.

"New Pledges of Kappa Chi Sorority," *The Jackson Sun*, September 22, 1953.

"New Type Phones Lighter, Smaller," *The Commercial Appeal*, February 19, 1960.

"Off to Hollywood," *Memphis Press-Scimitar*, September 7, 1957.

"One of These Beauties Destined for Hollywood Career," *New Orleans States*, August 30, 1957.

"One of These Will Be 'Miss Tennessee'," *The Jackson Sun*, July 26, 1956.

"Pick Winner Here Friday In Star Hunt Contest," *New Orleans States*, August 28, 1957.

Potts, Erwin, "Elvis' Old Flame Sports Sparkler," *Miami Herald*, April, 1959.

"Present From Elvis to Anita: A Diamond Necklace," *The Commercial Appeal*, April 1960.

"Presley Lends Anita a Car," *Memphis Press-Scimitar*, September 1957.

"Presley Loans Anita a Car," *Memphis Press-Scimitar*, September 26, 1957

"Presley Property," *The Daily Dunklin Democrat*, April 4, 1962.

"Press Club Names Cast For Show," *The Commercial Appeal*, April, 1960.

"Rollin' On the Rocket," *The Commercial Appeal*, July 12, 1960.

Scott, Vernon, "Ring 'Mighty Romantic' Even on Right Hand," *Memphis Press-Scimitar*, September 14, 1957.

"Singer Sidelined," *The Commercial Appeal*, October 1960.

"So Long, Elvis," *Memphis Press-Scimitar*, June 1958.

"Sparkling Array of Finalists in Mid-South Star Hunt," *Memphis Press-Scimitar*, August 23, 1957.

"Stepping Out...," *New York Journal-American*, 1958.

"Stubby Kaye Is Saturday Guest," *The Commercial Appeal*, Television Section, 1957.

Sublette, Bob, "Anita Credits States With Show Biz Break," *New Orleans States*, November 18, 1958.

"Sweet Sorrow," *The New York Post*, 1958.

Taylor, Audrey, "Skipper Elvis Splashes Off In His $2,500 Junior Yacht," *The Commercial Appeal*, July 9, 1960.

"Teen-Age Singer Turns D-J For 'Antics of Anita' Show," *The Jackson Sun*, 1955.

"The Biggest Show Ever Presented Jaycee Music Show," *The Daily Dunklin Democrat*, February 15, 1960.

"Theta Kappa Omega Acclaims Royalty," *The Jackson Sun*, June 20, 1954.

"Travel Togs for Two Movie Star Hopefuls," *Memphis Press-Scimitar*, August 28, 1957.

"Variety Show Slated By National Guard," *The Jackson Sun*, March 27, 1955.

"Versatile Anita Wood To Sing In Miss Nashville High Contest," *The Nashville Banner*, February 10, 1961.

White, James H., "Elvis Will Let Army Call Tune About His Singing," *Memphis Press-Scimitar*, June 1958.

Williams, Bob, "On The Air," *Memphis Press-Scimitar*, 1958.

Wilson, Earl, "It Happened Last Night," New York Post, August 8, 1958.

"Wink Martindale to Act as MC For '57 Miss Tennessee Pageant," *The Jackson Sun*, July 1957.

"Young Woman in a Shoe," *Memphis Press-Scimitar*, May 16, 1963.

"Youngster to Vie for Talent Honors," *The Commercial Appeal*, October 3, 1954.

Other Sources

Email correspondence from Wink Martindale, July 5, 2012.

Letter from Linda McDaniel, U.S. press respresentative for *Elvis Monthly* magazine, February 27, 1962.

CPSIA information can be obtained at www.ICGtesting.com
Printed in the USA
LVOW102043070713

341668LV00004B/4/P